The

Snake

An Owner's Guide To

A HAPPY HEALTHY PET

Howell Book House

Howell Book House
A Simon & Schuster Macmillan Company
1633 Broadway
New York, NY 10019

Library of Congress Cataloging-in-Publication Data
Flank, Lenny.
The Snake/by Lenny Flank.
p. cm.—(An owner's guide to a happy healthy pet)

ISBN 0-87605-490-4

1. Snakes as pets.   I. Title.   II. Series.
SF459.S5F58   1996
639.3'96—DC20   96-23745
                    CIP

Manufactured in the United States of America
10 9 8 7 6 5 4 3 2 1

Series Director: Dominique De Vito
Series Assistant Editor: Ariel Cannon
Book Design: Michele Laseau
Cover Design: Iris Jeromnimon
Illustration: Laura Robbins
Photography:
  Cover: Bill Love
  Joan Balzarini: 16, 27, 30, 34, 44, 58, 64, 86, 89, 90, 94, 114, 118
  Lenny Flank: 53, 55, 66, 67, 96
  Bill Love: 2–3, 5, 6, 7, 8, 9, 10, 11, 13, 14, 17, 18, 19, 20, 22, 23, 24, 25, 26, 28, 29, 31, 32, 33, 35, 36, 37, 38, 39, 40, 42, 46, 48–49, 50, 52, 59, 71, 72, 78, 81, 82, 83, 84, 85, 87, 88, 91, 93, 97, 98–99, 100, 101, 103, 104, 106, 107, 108, 110, 111, 112, 115, 116, 117
Production Team: Kathleen Caulfield, Vic Peterson, and Chris Van Camp

Contents

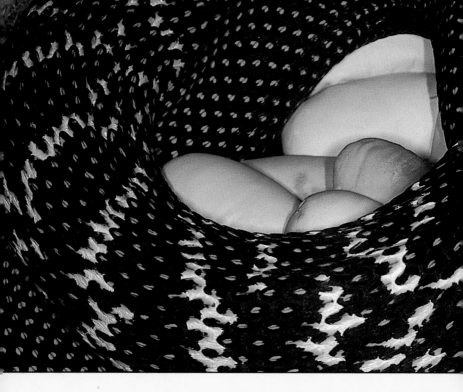

Snakes
and Their

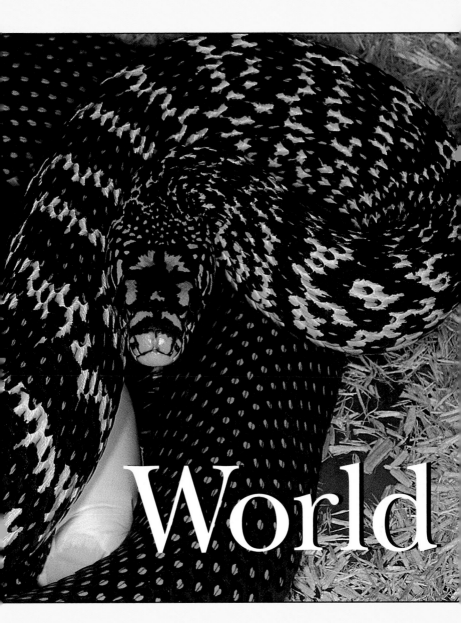

part one

World

Physical Features of the Snake

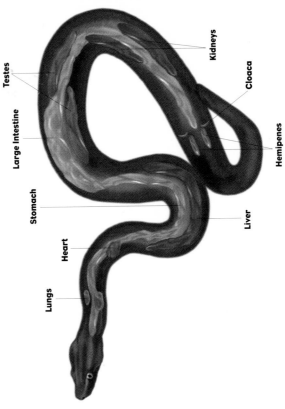

Lungs
Heart
Stomach
Large Intestine
Testes
Kidneys
Cloaca
Hemipenes
Liver

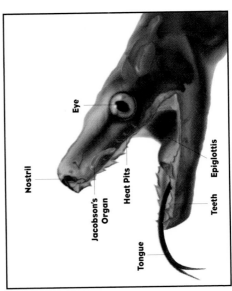

Nostril
Eye
Jacobson's Organ
Heat Pits
Teeth
Epiglottis
Tongue

chapter 1

What
Is a
Snake?

Just a few years ago, the very idea of keeping a snake as a pet in one's home would have sent shivers down the spines of most people. Today, however, we have become more ecologically aware, our knowledge of snakes and reptiles has expanded, and the number of people

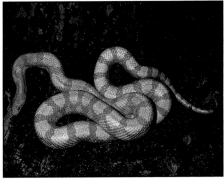

who have developed an interest in these fascinating animals has grown enormously.

It has been estimated that some 7 percent of all American families—over two million people—have at least one reptile, usually a snake, they keep as a pet. Herpetoculture, the keeping of snakes and other reptiles in captivity, is one of the fastest-growing hobbies in the country. Several million reptiles are imported each year, most destined to be pets. A number of magazines, books and even computer networks

Snakes and
Their World

devoted solely to this hobby have appeared in recent
years.

Snakes Are Reptiles

There are about 2,700 species of snakes in existence
today. These animals have adapted to a wide variety

of habitats, from steaming
tropical jungles to hot, arid
deserts, to cool temperate
climates near the arctic
circle. All snakes are reptiles, which are characterized by the following traits:
dry scaly skin; a depen-
dence upon external heat
sources rather than internal
metabolism; and birthing
usually by a shelled egg that

*A distinguish-
ing character-
istic of snakes
is that they lay
shelled eggs on
land.* (Grey
Banded King)

can be laid on land. A few reptiles, such as boas, are
able to bear their young live without laying eggs. The
scientific study of reptiles (and amphibians) is called
herpetology, and reptiles and amphibians are usually
referred to collectively as "herpetofauna" or "herptiles," which is usually shortened in conversation to
"herps."

Like all other reptiles and amphibians, snakes are
"ectothermic," which means they cannot produce their
own internal body heat. In some older books, this is
referred to as being "cold-blooded," but this is not a
very accurate term, since some snakes can maintain
body temperatures of over 100 degrees—higher than
human temperature. The word "ectothermic" comes
from Latin words meaning "outside heat," which better
describes how the snake's metabolism functions.

Ectotherms, however, cannot produce enough body
heat metabolically to maintain their body temperatures at the desired level; if heating were left to their
metabolism alone, they would take on the same temperature as their surroundings. To prevent this, and to
maintain a suitable body temperature, reptiles must

use external sources of heat to keep their internal temperatures high enough. That is why snakes and lizards are most often seen basking in the sun; they are using the heat provided by the sun to raise their body temperatures to an acceptable level.

This need to maintain and conserve body heat is one of the most important factors in any snake's life. In hot, tropical environments such as Latin America and Africa, it is easy for the snake to maintain a high body temperature, and tropical jungles are usually teeming with a wide variety of snakes. In addition, because the ambient temperature is so high, tropical snakes can afford to develop large, heavy bodies, which would take an unacceptably long time to warm up if such snakes lived in cooler areas.

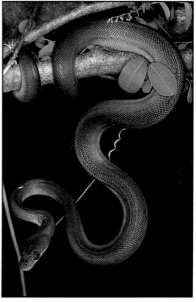

In cooler temperate regions like North America and Europe, it is more difficult for a snake to stay warm. As a result, snakes from cooler areas are typically smaller and darker in color than tropical snakes. (This size and coloration allow them to absorb sunlight and warm up faster.) In the winter, when short days and colder temperatures make it impossible to keep the preferred body temperature, snakes retreat to underground chambers and hibernate, shutting down virtually all of their bodily functions, including enzyme activity. The snakes emerge in the spring when the days grow longer and the temperature gets warmer.

Because snakes cannot control their own body temperatures, they are most commonly found in warm, tropical areas. (Olive Python)

How Snakes Move

The most immediately apparent characteristic of snakes, of course, is the fact that they have no legs. It is a common belief that snakes walk on the ends of their ribs, but this is not true. Instead, the snake uses special sets of muscles attached to the ribs to lift the large rectangular belly scales off the ground and pull them forward. Once the loose edges of these scales have caught on the irregularities in the ground, these muscles contract and pull the snake forward, using the scales as anchoring points. If the snake is placed on a totally smooth surface such as a piece of glass, there are no irregularities for the belly scales to catch, and the snake will not be able to move forward.

Because of their long, thin bodies, snakes are excellent climbers, able to contort themselves into all kinds of positions. (Grey Rat Snake)

Because of their long, thin bodies, most snakes are excellent climbers. Because their spines are long and supple, snakes can contort themselves into the most difficult positions to gain purchase on a branch or rock face. An average snake may have over 200 vertebrae in its body, each attached to its neighbor by special bony spines and a ball-and-socket joint. While each individual joint in the backbone can only flex a little, the large number of joints allows the snake to move with fluidity and suppleness.

The Snake's Anatomy

THE SKULL

The bones in a snake's skull suit their specialized feeding habits. Since a snake does not have chewing teeth and also has no limbs to help it hold or tear prey, all food must be swallowed whole.

An average snake can swallow prey up to three times the diameter of its head—the equivalent of a human swallowing a basketball whole. To accomplish this feat, the bones of the snake's skull are very loosely connected by flexible ligaments. The jaw can be dislocated, separating from the skull to produce an enormous gape, and the two halves of the jawbone can also be spread widely apart at the chin. During feeding, the brain is protected by a bony box at the rear of the skull. After the food has been swallowed, you will see your snake yawn widely once or twice to help put its jaw bones back in place.

THE TEETH

Snakes have many more teeth than humans or other mammals. Most species of snakes have over 200 teeth, which are found in two rows along the roof of the mouth, as well as around the rims of both upper and lower jaws. Unlike a mammal's, a snake's teeth are not set in sockets; instead, they are attached to the sides of the jawbones, an arrangement known technically as *pleurodont* teeth.

Most species of snakes have over 200 teeth, all the same size and shape. (African Bush Viper)

Except for the fangs in venomous species and a few elongated teeth in some arboreal boids, all of a snake's teeth are of the same size and shape. Snakes do not have the differently shaped incisors, canines and molars found in mammals. Snake teeth are relatively long and curve backwards towards the throat, helping to hold struggling prey while it is being killed and swallowed. Snakes cannot use their teeth to chew.

Snake teeth continuously fall out and are replaced as the snake grows. This insures that the teeth are always sharp, and that broken teeth can be quickly replaced. Even the hollow fangs of the venomous species are periodically replaced by a fresh set.

THE EYES

The anatomy of the snake's eyes differs from that of most other vertebrates. Other vertebrates are able to focus a sharp image on the retina of their eyes, by using special muscles to change the shape of the lens. In snakes, however, these muscles are absent, and the snake can only focus an image by moving the whole lens back and forth. As a result, snakes have extremely poor vision, and cannot separate stationary objects from the background. They are, however, very sensitive to movement.

THE JACOBSON'S ORGAN

Since snakes have such poor eyesight, they depend largely upon their sensitivity to chemical signals to locate their prey and to find breeding partners. You will often see your snake continuously flicking out its long forked tongue; the frequency of this tongue-darting increases when the snake finds something of interest. The surface of the snake's tongue picks up microscopic scent particles in the air and transfers

Snakes depend on their tongues to give them information about their environment. (Leucistic Texas Rat Snake)

them to the Jacobson's Organ in the roof of its mouth, which is connected directly to the brain through the olfactory nerve. This chemical sampling, which functions like a cross between the senses of taste and smell, provides the snake with most of its information regarding its surroundings.

THE HEAT PITS

Several groups of snakes have developed infrared-sensitive pits at the front of the face, which can detect the body heat of warm-blooded animals. In boas and pythons, these take the form of a row of pits in the upper lip; in the pit vipers, they consist of two openings on either side of the face. In both cases, the pit consists of a deep hollow with a very thin membrane of skin stretched across it. This thin membrane is filled with a large number of nerve endings.

You can clearly see the heat pits on this Nose-Horned Viper.

These structures are extremely sensitive to heat, and can detect changes in temperature as small as one-eighth of a degree Fahrenheit. Snakes that possess these pits feed upon warm-blooded prey such as rodents or birds, and sense their presence by detecting these animals' body heat. Because the pits are located on both sides of the face, snakes that have them can compare the perceived heat intensity from one side with the other, and thus triangulate the position of the heat source. Boas and pythons can locate and strike at prey using their facial pits even if they have been blindfolded.

WHAT IS A SNAKE?

A snake is a limbless reptile, characterized by its dry, scaly skin; dependence upon external heat sources rather than internal metabolism (ectothermic); and ability to lay shelled eggs (some even bear live young).

Scientifically, snakes belong in the suborder Serpentes, from the order Squamata (which means scaled).

THE BRAIN

The structure of a snake's brain is somewhat similar to that of a bird, but the snake, like all reptiles, lacks the enlarged cerebral hemispheres found in birds and mammals. Since the cerebrum is the part of the brain that controls learning and thought, snakes are not as

Snakes and
Their World

intelligent as birds or mammals. They are capable of a fair amount of learning, however, and can even retain some memories for as long as several weeks. Captive snakes will very quickly learn when their regularly scheduled feeding time is, for instance, and will often be ready and waiting when their owner approaches with food. Although pet snakes can distinguish human beings from other types of animals, it is not known whether they can learn to tell their owner from other human beings.

ARE SNAKES SMART?

Snakes, like all reptiles, lack the enlarged cerebral hemispheres found in birds and mammals—the part of the brain that controls learning and thought. Consequently, snakes are not what we would consider intelligent. They are creatures of instinct and habit. Captive snakes will learn when their regularly scheduled feeding time is, and their owners will often find them waiting. They have no emotions as we know them, though they certainly feel things, such as pain.

THE LUNGS

Since the lungs of a snake must fit inside a narrow elongated body, their structure is somewhat different from those of most animals. In most snakes, the right lung is large, and extends for almost a third of the body length. The left lung, by contrast, is greatly reduced in size, and may even be completely absent in some species. In effect, snakes have only one lung.

During feeding, when the mouth may be blocked for up to an hour by food, the snake is able to breathe by extending a muscular extension of its windpipe, called the epiglottis, from the bottom of the mouth. It protrudes from underneath the prey to reach air and allow the snake to breathe.

THE HEART

Like nearly all reptiles (with the exception of the crocodilians), snakes have a primitive three-chambered heart that is not as efficient as the four-chambered hearts found in mammals. In snakes, the blood is pumped to the lungs by one of the two upper chambers, known as atria, and returns to the single lower ventricle, where it mixes with the oxygen-depleted blood that is returning from the rest of the body. This

12

mixture of oxygen-rich and oxygen-depleted blood is then pumped into the other atrium, where it enters the aortic arches and is distributed throughout the body. Because of this inefficient method of distributing oxygen, even the most active snakes tire easily, and cannot sustain activity for any length of time without frequent stops for rest.

THE SKIN

Snake skin consists of two layers. The inner layer contains the nerve endings and the color pigment cells. The outer layer consists of large oval scales, which overlap each other like the shingles on a roof. These scales are made of keratin, the same protein from which human fingernails are made.

The shedding skin of this Florida King Snake shows the dead outer layer coming off of the new inner layer.

The outer layer of a snake's skin is dead and cannot grow. As the snake grows larger, therefore, the old skin becomes tighter and tighter, and the snake must remove it in order to increase its size. This process of shedding the skin is called *ecdysis*. Shortly before the shed takes place, the snake secretes a fluid between the two layers of skin, and grows a new keratin layer underneath the old one. This fluid causes the snake's colors to turn dark, and also makes the eyes look blue. The snake will then rub its nose and lips on a rock or other hard surface until the old skin layer is broken, and then crawls completely out of the old skin, which turns inside out and is removed in one long piece.

THE STOMACH

The snake's stomach is very muscular and elastic, and can expand enormously to contain the large prey animals eaten by snakes. The digestive juices are powerful: Nearly the entire prey is digested, including most of the bones and teeth. Because their food requirements are low and their digestive system is very efficient, snakes can go for long periods on a single meal.

THE KIDNEYS

Snakes have very large kidneys in proportion to their body size. These are staggered in the snake's abdominal region, the left kidney behind the right one. The kidneys filter waste products and toxins from the bloodstream and pass them on to the cloaca for elimination. Unlike mammals, which excrete nitrogen wastes in the form of water-soluble urea, snakes excrete these body wastes as crystals of uric acid, which form a dry white paste and are expelled along with the feces. This process allows snakes to be extremely efficient in their use of water.

THE CLOACA

Unlike mammals, snakes do not have separate urinary, reproductive and anal openings. Instead, the urinary, digestive and reproductive tracts all empty into a common chamber called the cloaca (this arrangement is also found in birds). Digestive waste products are stored here until they can be eliminated. The cloaca opens to the

---

DID YOU KNOW?

The scientific study of reptiles and amphibians is called herpetology, and the animals themselves are herptiles, commonly shortened to herps.

Snakes have no eyelids; instead, their eyes are protected by a hard, clear scale called a brille, or eye-cap.

Snakes don't have ears and are completely deaf to airborne sounds, but they do pick up vibrations through their jawbones and scent molecules on their tongues. The scent molecules are transmitted through the mouth to the Jacobson's Organ, and then translated in the brain to tell snakes about their environment.

Snakes move by using special muscles attached to their ribs, and scales on their bellies that act as anchors. A snake cannot move forward on a smooth piece of glass because there's nothing to grab on to.

Snakes can swallow food up to three times the diameter of their head. That's like you or me being able to swallow a basketball!

Most snakes have over 200 teeth—many more than humans and other mammals.

outside through a transverse slit just behind the snake's tail.

Some snakes also have a number of special defensive glands which empty into the cloaca. These glands contain a foul-smelling musk which can be ejected whenever the snake is threatened or disturbed.

THE HEMIPENES

Like most reptiles, all snakes practice internal fertilization, in which sperm are introduced directly into the female's cloaca. Instead of a penis, male snakes possess a pair of copulatory organs called hemipenes, which are covered with a particular pattern of spines and knobs. These spines help lock the male into position during breeding. During the mating process, only one of the pair of hemipenes is actually used.

In temperate areas, male snakes produce sperm during their period of hibernation. The sperm in species from temperate climates requires a cooler temperature to mature properly, and if the male is kept artificially warm and not allowed to hibernate, the sperm will be killed by the abnormal heat. This will render the male incapable of breeding during the spring.

During mating, one pair of male hemipenes enters the female cloaca. (Cal Kings)

chapter 2

Fossil
History
of Snakes

Snakes are the most recent of the groups of reptiles to appear. While the reptiles as a whole are a very ancient group, predating the dinosaurs, snakes do not make their appearance in the fossil record until just before the dinosaurs became extinct, some seventy million years ago. Despite their relatively recent development, however, the fossil history of snakes is very poorly known because snake skeletons are very delicate and do not fossilize easily.

The Evolution of Reptiles

According to most paleontologists, reptiles evolved from the large group of ancient amphibians known as *Labrynthodonts*, which received their name from the distinctive structure of their teeth. In the Labrynthodonts, the enamel of the tooth was folded in on itself to form a complex, maze-like pattern.

What set reptiles apart from amphibians was their ability to lay shelled eggs. (Elaphe carinata)

The evolutionary advance that set the reptiles apart from the amphibians was the development of the amniote or shelled egg, which could be laid on land, freeing the reptiles from the necessity of returning to the water as adults for reproduction. The oldest known fossil egg was found in Texas, and dates from the lower Permian period of the earth's history (over 275 million years ago).

The oldest fossil that can be definitely recognized as a reptile is a small, lizard-like animal known as *Hylonomus*, whose skeleton has been found inside petrified tree stumps in Nova Scotia. During the period of time in which *Hylonomus* lived, the earth was a different place than it is now. The continents were all joined into one large super-continent known as Pangea ("all earth"), and even such places as Antarctica and northern Canada had warm, humid climates and lush, tropical forests.

THE EVOLUTION OF SNAKES

From fossil records, scientists have been able to determine that snakes evolved just before the extinction of the dinosaurs, some 70 million years ago. Because snakes are so closely related to reptiles, and some dinosaurs were reptilian, snakes are distantly related to some dinosaurs, most notably the Tyrannosaurus and Triceratops.

The earliest snake to appear in the fossil record, *Lapparentophis defrenni*, dates from the early Cretaceous period, about 130 million years ago.

Pythons and boas are the most ancient of modern snakes.

Hylonomus was a member of a group of very ancient reptiles known as the *Cotylosaurs,* or stem reptiles, which are believed by paleontologists to be ancestors of all of the reptile families alive today. The Cotylosaurs first appeared during the Permian, the period that immediately preceded the rise of the dinosaurs.

*Boas and pythons
are usually con-
sidered to be the
most primitive of
the living snakes.*
(Madagascar
Tree Boa)

During the next few million years, the Cotylosaurs divided into three distinct groups of reptiles, which are distinguished from each other by their differing skull structures. The earliest of the Cotylosaurs were Anapsids, which means that they lacked any arches or openings between their skull bones.

The Anapsids eventually went on to produce the modern turtles. Later, another group of Cotylosaurs developed a single arch in the skull, between the postorbital and squamosal bones, through which the jaw muscles passed. These reptiles are known as Synapsids, and they went on to evolve into the modern mammals.

The third group of reptiles, the Diapsids, divided to produce both the dinosaurs as well as the modern lizards and snakes. Thus, though snakes are not direct descendants of the dinosaurs, they are evolutionary cousins of Tyrannosaurus and Triceratops.

Scientists have concluded that the snakes probably evolved from a family of lizards during the time of the dinosaurs. Snakes and lizards share a number of distinct features in their skull structure; for example, both possess a moveable quadrate bone at the back of the jaw, and both are missing the quadratojugal bone at the rear of the skull. In particular, the Varanid family of lizards, which includes the monitor lizards, are very similar to snakes in their skull structure.

From Burrowing to Slithering

Based on these similarities, herpetologists have theorized that an ancient group of monitor-like lizards began to follow a burrowing way of life, tunneling through loose dirt and sand in search of earthworms and other prey (just as some lizards do today). Over a period of millions of years, these burrowing lizards lost their limbs and their external ears—to help them burrow more easily—and also replaced their eyelids with a clear brille or spectacle to protect their eyes while digging.

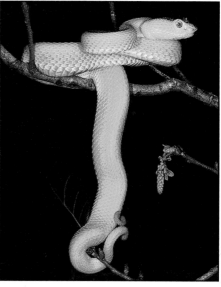

At about the time that the dinosaurs died out, one group of these burrowing lizards gave up its subterranean lifestyle and emerged to the surface, where they then developed a new legless mode of locomotion. They rapidly diversified, invading a large number of ecological niches. Today we classify the various descendants of these legless lizards as snakes.

Vipers, the most highly specialized snakes, appeared about ten million years ago. (Gold Eyelash Viper)

chapter 3

Choosing
a Snake

Probably the most common question asked by the beginning herper is, "Which kind of snake should I get?" This can also be one of the most difficult questions to answer. It depends upon several factors, including personal preference as to color and size; how much space one can dedicate to keeping the snake; what sort of climatic conditions one can provide; how often one intends to handle the snake; and whether or not one already has other snakes. These are just a few of the concerns of the snake keeper.

Qualities of a Suitable Snake

In general, a suitable snake for a beginning herper should (1) be docile and tame, and easy to handle; (2) be of a medium size;

(3) have a diet that can be easily provided; and (4) be tolerant of a wide range of environmental factors.

Very often, financial considerations must be acknowledged as well. While some snakes, such as garter snakes or green snakes, are very inexpensive, others that also make excellent pets, such as Rainbow or Rosy Boas are only rarely bred in captivity and are quite expensive. Some snakes can be fed a steady diet of earthworms or goldfish, which can be obtained cheaply in any pet store, while others may require more expensive food such as chickens or rabbits, which will probably have to be special-ordered. Since most snakes have lifespans of almost twenty years, it is important to choose a snake that you can afford to care for over a period of decades.

The 10 Best—And Worst— Snakes

Keeping all of these factors in mind, here is my personal list of the 10 best—and 10 worst—snakes to keep as pets:

THE 10 BEST

I. Corn Snakes *(Elaphe guttata)*

Among experienced snake keepers, this is nearly a unanimous choice for the best pet for a beginning herper. Corn snakes, which are native to the southeastern United States, reach a maximum length of around five feet and are very docile, and can be easily tamed and handled. They are reliable feeders, and will readily accept mice (which can be found in any pet store). They can tolerate a wide range of environmental conditions and aren't very fussy about heat and light requirements.

They are also available in a wide range of strikingly beautiful color patterns. Naturally-colored corn snakes are reddish brown with a pattern of large, darker splotches along the back, and attractive red and black checkers along the belly. Other color patterns, which

21

have been artificially bred, include the Snow Corn, which is pale in color with darker blotches, and the Okeetee or Orange Corn, which has the same basic pattern as the natural snake but with much brighter orange colors. Albino corn snakes are also readily available.

*Snow Corn
Snake.*

*Everglades Rat
Snake.*

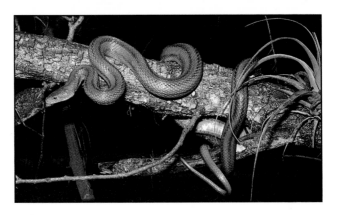

2. Rat Snakes *(Elaphe species)*

The rat snakes are a wide-ranging group of snakes found in North America, Europe and Asia. In size and appearance, they are very similar to the corn snake—which is not surprising, since the corn snake itself is a member of the rat snake family, and is often sold as the "Red Rat Snake."

Like the corn snakes, rat snakes are good-natured and adaptable, and do very well in captivity. They feed readily on rodent prey. Among the species of rat snake you are likely to find on dealers' lists are the Black Rat Snake, the Yellow Rat Snake and the Grey Rat Snake. All are excellent pets.

3. King Snakes *(Lampropeltus getulus)*

There are several different varieties of king snake available in the pet trade, all of them attractively patterned. The most commonly available are the Common or Chain King Snake, which is glossy black with a network of thin yellow or white stripes; the Florida or Speckled King Snake, which is black or dark blue with numerous tiny white or yellow spots; and the California King Snake, which is black or dark blue with wide white or yellow crossbands. All of these varieties are subspecies and can interbreed with each other.

South Florida King Snake.

King snakes average about six feet long and are a bit more heavy-bodied than the rat snakes. They are alert and active, and tame readily. They are also not demanding in regard to environmental conditions, and can adapt to a wide range of humidity and temperature. Although most of their food in the wild consists of other reptiles, they will happily accept a diet of mice and other rodents.

There is one major drawback to the king snake, however: It is a confirmed snake-eater, and earned its name because it is capable of overpowering and eating nearly any other snake, including the venomous

23

rattlesnakes. Even a middling-sized king snake will be able to attack, constrict and swallow a much larger snake by carefully folding the victim up inside the stomach as it is being swallowed. King snakes must therefore be kept individually in separate cages—to a king snake, another king snake, even a sibling, is just as acceptable fare as any other snake would be.

*Albino Milk
Snake.*

4. Milk Snakes *(Lampropeltus triangulum)*

Few animals are as spectacularly colored as are some of the milk snakes. The basic color scheme consists of alternating bands of bright red, yellow and black, and these startling reptiles are often referred to as "Candy-Cane Snakes." The colors are a defense mechanism; they closely mimic the pattern of the dangerously venomous Coral Snake, and thus fool potential predators into leaving the milk snake alone.

The Honduran and the Sinaloan Milk Snakes are the races most commonly found in the pet trade, as they have the most spectacular colors. In addition to their extremely attractive colors, milk snakes are hardy and docile, and do very well in captivity. They are a very good snake for a beginning herper.

There is only one disadvantage to the milk snakes; they are closely related to the king snakes, and like them, milk snakes are confirmed snake eaters. Although as pets they will readily accept mice and other rodents as food, milk snakes cannot be kept together, or one snake will eventually make lunch out of its cagemate.

5. Garter Snakes *(Thamnophis sirtalis)* and Ribbon Snakes *(Thamnophis sauritus)*

These two very common North American snakes are closely related and share many environmental and food requirements. They look so much alike that it may be extremely difficult to tell them apart. I have therefore lumped them together in this list.

Checkered Garter Snake.

Garter and ribbon snakes are two of the most widespread snakes in the world. They range from northern Mexico almost to the Arctic Circle in Canada. Not surprisingly, they are very tolerant of a wide range of environmental conditions; they are tough, resilient snakes which can take less than ideal conditions and still thrive. They also do not get very big—usually less than three feet—and tame quickly. And, because they breed very readily in captivity, they are widely available and are very inexpensive.

Another point in these snakes' favor is that, unlike most pet snakes, they do not need to be fed rodent food. Garter snakes will thrive on a diet of earthworms and goldfish. Ribbon snakes do not normally eat earthworms, but will accept goldfish, minnows and small frogs.

All in all, these snakes are tough, undemanding and very inexpensive to maintain. They are an excellent choice for the beginning snake keeper.

6. Pine Snakes and Bull Snakes *(Pituophis melanoleucus)*

The pine snake and the bull snake are geographical groups of the same species. The pine snake is found in the temperate forests of the southeastern United States, while the bull snake is adapted for the arid semi-deserts of the American West. They are very similar in their care requirements, with the bull snake requiring somewhat higher temperatures than its eastern cousin.

Florida Pine Snake.

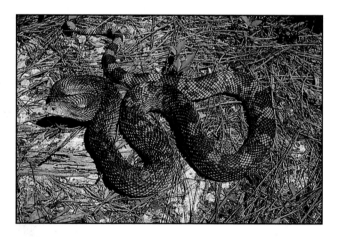

Bull and pine snakes are large, averaging around six feet and sometimes reaching eight feet. They are also much more heavy-bodied than a corn or rat snake, and are very powerfully muscled. When handled, both pine snakes and bull snakes have a habit of wrapping around your arm and tightening their grip until it feels as though your hand will fall off, and then relaxing and moving off. Why they do this is not known, but it certainly demonstrates the sheer power that these snakes have.

When confronted in the wild, both varieties will rear their heads off the ground, vibrate the tip of the tail rapidly, and let out an extremely loud and long rattling hiss, which is enough to scare off all but the most determined of predators. Wild-caught individuals tend to be defensive and nervous, and will often hiss and strike at their keepers, but the strikes are usually made with the mouth closed. It is rare for a bull or pine snake to actually attempt to bite. In captivity, they become tame very quickly, and soon are hardy and active pets.

Ball Python.

7. Ball Python *(Python regius)*

The Ball Python, known in Europe as the Royal Python, is extremely popular in the pet trade, and tens of thousands of them are sold each year. They are very attractively patterned, with large black or chocolate brown markings on a tan or light brown background.

Although the Ball Python is extremely heavy-bodied and weighs a lot for its size, it is one of the smallest of the boids, and rarely exceeds four-and-a-half feet in length. They are not aggressive snakes at all, and seldom try to bite. When frightened, they may coil their bodies into a tight ball and tuck their heads inside—a habit which they soon give up in captivity.

Because of their manageable size and their docile temperament, they make very good pets, provided that suitable conditions can be maintained. Like all boids, Ball Pythons need high temperatures and high humidity to thrive, and are susceptible to a variety of health problems if these conditions are not maintained. They can also be problem feeders, and are prone to stop eating for distressingly long periods of time and for no apparent reason. Thus, although they make excellent pets, my recommendation would be to obtain a Ball Python as a second snake, after you already have some snake-keeping experience to your credit.

Mexican Rosy Boa.

8. Rosy Boa *(Lichanura trivirgata)*

Looking at this little snake (three feet long) with its attractively striped pattern, it is hard to believe that it is closely related to some of the largest snakes in the Western Hemisphere. Yet the little Rosy Boa belongs to the same group of snakes as the Boa Constrictor and the Anaconda. It is, in fact, one of the smallest boids in the world, and is found in California and Mexico.

The Rosy Boa is an inhabitant of arid semi-desert grasslands, where it feeds upon mice and lizards, which it kills by constriction—just like its larger cousins. It does well in captivity, provided that its environmental demands—warm, dry conditions—can be met.

Since the Rosy Boa is somewhat rare in the wild, it has been legally protected by the State of California. As a result, it is not widely bred, and finding a specimen may be difficult (you can expect to pay top dollar for it if you do find it). Nevertheless, it is a very interesting snake which is not at all difficult to keep.

9. Rainbow Boa *(Epicrates species)*

For many snake keepers, the Rainbow Boa is the holy grail to which they aspire. These medium-sized (up to five or six feet) boids from Latin America are quite possibly the most beautifully colored snakes on earth, with a spectacular display of iridescent, multi-colored patterns on a bright orange background.

Although they are a bit more defensive than the more common Boa Constrictor, Rainbow Boas tame readily if they are obtained young and handled often. In the wild, they feed largely on nestling birds and eggs, but captives will happily feed on mice and other rodents. They need warm and extremely humid environmental conditions.

A newborn Brazilian Rainbow Boa.

Unfortunately, however, Rainbows are not widely bred and are therefore rather expensive (anywhere from $100 to over $500 for a young snake, depending on the species). There are two varieties of Rainbow Boa. The more common Columbian Rainbow Boa has the typical spectacular color pattern as a youngster, but gradually fades with age to a uniform chocolate brown color. The Brazilian variety, on the other hand, retains its brilliant coloration throughout adulthood. The Brazilian species, therefore, can cost several times as much as its Columbian cousin. These animals are rather pricey and somewhat delicate for a first snake, but definitely worth considering as an addition to your collection.

10. Red Tailed Boa *(Boa constrictor)*

This is probably the most famous snake in the world, but its reported size and aggressiveness are greatly

exaggerated. Despite what you may hear, Boa Constrictors are not the longest of the snakes; in fact, they
do not even rank in the top five. An average Boa
Constrictor will reach a length of around ten feet,
although exceptional individuals may get up to fifteen
or eighteen feet. They will weigh around seventy-five or
so pounds.

Red Tailed Boa.

Although this is a middling size among the big boids, a
ten-foot snake is still pretty impressive. While this boa
is justifiably popular in the pet trade because of its
placid disposition and attractive silver-and-brown color
scheme, a full-grown individual may be difficult to handle without help. You will also be forking out a lot of
cash to house and feed a big boa. Nevertheless, boas
are tough and undemanding snakes that can be cared
for easily. If you absolutely must have a large boid, the
Boa Constrictor is probably your best choice, but start
out with a very young one.

THE 10 WORST

I. Any Venomous Snake

Although it should go without saying that any dangerously venomous snake is not suitable as a pet, there are
unfortunately a number of dealers and breeders who
will sell such highly dangerous serpents as cobras, vipers
and rattlesnakes. In fact, almost half of all the snakebites
reported in the United States each year are the result of

improper handling of pet snakes. Since this book is intended for the beginning snake hobbyist, it should be doubly stressed that venomous or hot snakes are not pets and should not be kept under any circumstances.

One of the most vigorous debates in the hobby of snake keeping today, however, concerns the question of de-venomed or venomoid snakes. These are venomous species such as cobras, copperheads and rattlesnakes that have been surgically altered by a veterinarian, sometimes by removing the venom sacs completely using a laser, but more usually by making a small slit in the side of the snake's cheek and severing the duct leading from the snake's venom sac to the fang. This has the effect of rendering that particular snake incapable of injecting its venom.

Spectacled Cobra.

Are these de-venomed snakes safe? They are unable to inject any venom and do not present any danger of poisoning the owner; however, though the venom ducts have been cut, the snake still possesses a full complement of fangs. The fangs cannot be permanently removed because, like all of the snake's teeth, they are constantly replaced during life. So, even though that four-foot Gaboon Viper cannot inject any venom, he can still strike and bite with his inch-and-a-half fangs, and such a bite is nothing to trifle with. While some de-venomed snakes (particularly Elapids, such as cobras) may become tame enough to handle, many will remain nervous and defensive, and are apt to strike at their keeper.

The proponents of de-venomed snakes make the argument that such a process allows serious herpers to keep and own some of the most fascinating snakes in the world without the dangers inherent in venomous animals. Opponents of keeping "venomoid" snakes point out that: (1) a snake's venom is important to the process of digestion, and removing the venom may affect the health of the snake; and (2) it is cruel and unnecessary to subject a snake to a surgical procedure simply for human vanity and machismo. It should also be noted that, in some jurisdictions that have outlawed keeping venomous snakes (see chapter 8), the fact that the snake is de-venomed may not change its legal status.

Rhinoceros Viper.

My own opinion is that the only justification for surgically altering a venomous snake is when the animal is to be used for educational purposes (lectures and talks), where safety considerations and insurance problems make using "hot" snakes impractical or undesirable. For this reason, I must place the de-venomed snakes, along with the fully venomous examples, at the top of my worst snakes list.

2. Any Wild-Caught Snake

As the number of people enjoying the hobby of snake keeping has grown, however, so too have the pressures exerted upon native populations of snakes by collectors who capture wild snakes for the pet trade. This situation only adds to the already crushing problems of loss of habitat and environmental pollution. As a result, the populations of many species of snake have plummeted drastically.

Fortunately, a wide variety of snakes are now being bred in captivity and farm-raised by professional and amateur breeders, doing away with the necessity of taking any more animals from the wild. These captive-bred animals are also healthier and have better dispositions than wild-caught snakes.

Before you buy any snake, please check and make sure that it was captive-bred and not taken from the wild. And if you ever see a snake in the woods, resist the temptation to add it to your collection; leave it in the wild for future generations to enjoy.

Reticulated Python.

3. Reticulated Python *(Python reticulatus)*

When it comes to particular species to avoid, the Reticulated Python is at the top of everybody's list. Nearly every experienced snake keeper has a horror story to tell about being bitten by one of these snakes (the best description that I've ever heard of the Retic's disposition is, "like the Grinch with a bad case of hemorrhoids").

The Reticulated Python is the longest snake in the world, and can reach lengths of up to thirty-three feet.

Although individual snakes may be calm and docile, most are temperamental, unpredictable and irritable. This is the only snake in the world that has been reliably confirmed to have killed and eaten human beings, and over the years several zoo keepers have been killed by large captive Retics. Fortunately, Reticulated Pythons seem to be less common in the pet trade than they used to be. They are not a snake for an inexperienced herper.

4. Burmese Python *(Python molurus bivittatus)*

These snakes are, unfortunately, extremely common in the pet trade, and nearly every pet store you are likely to visit will have two or three brightly colored Burmese Python hatchlings. Their appeal is also increased by the fact that they have been bred in several quite attractive color patterns, including albinos. And, because they breed readily in captivity, they are relatively inexpensive to obtain.

*Albino Burmese
Python.*

Despite their attractiveness and their relatively docile natures, however, Burmese Pythons are a good snake for a beginner to avoid. Within two or three years, that cute little 2-foot hatchling you brought home will be a 15-foot, 120-pound monster with an endless appetite, gulping down chickens and rabbits as fast as you can acquire them (he'll also gulp down the family dog or cat if he can catch it). Usually, an entire room of the house must be devoted to meeting this snake's needs. And, since a Burmese Python can live for over twenty years, this will be a lifelong commitment. Save this one until you have a lot of snake experience under your belt (and a lot of room in your house).

5. Anaconda *(Eunectes murinus)*

The Anaconda, which at 30 feet and 200 pounds is the heaviest (though not the longest) snake in the world, can give the Reticulated Python a good run for its money for the title of "world's nastiest snake." Although the rare individual can be taught to tolerate handling, most of these snakes are irascible and unpredictable, and will bite on a moment's notice. In the wild, they routinely polish off critters that are a lot tougher than you are, including full-grown caimans and jaguars.

Yellow Anaconda.

Anacondas are also difficult to provide with adequate housing, since they spend most of their time in water— a large specimen will need a room of its own with a built-in swimming pool to be properly cared for.

Fortunately, these monsters are rare in the pet trade (breeders and dealers don't like to handle them either). Some dealers offer the related Yellow Anaconda. It's not as big, but is just as nasty as its cousin.

6. Green Snakes *(Opheodrys species)*

These beautiful snakes, with their long, slender bodies (up to four feet) and their attractive lemon-lime color scheme, are very common in the pet trade, and are inexpensive to boot. Unfortunately, they are extremely delicate, and even experienced snake keepers will have

35

Snakes and
Their World

difficulty in keeping them alive for more than a few months.

Part of the problem lies in their specialized food requirements. Unlike most snakes, green snakes are entirely insectivorous, and will usually eat only soft-bodied, hairless catepillars. Since this food is of rather low quality, they must be fed more often than other snakes.

Western Smooth Green Snake.

7. Hog-Nose Snakes *(Heterodon species)*

These snakes are perhaps most famous for their elaborate "bluffing" ritual, which they perform whenever they feel threatened. The act begins with a loud prolonged hissing, caused by air being passed rapidly over the epiglottis. At the same time, the Hog-Nose will flatten the ribs of its neck just like a cobra, and will lunge violently at the perceived threat—always with mouth closed.

If, after a few threatening strikes, the danger does not go away, the Hog-Nose will then switch tactics. Now, it will suddenly begin to writhe and thrash about as if it were in unbearable agony, finishing by flopping over onto its back, opening its mouth, and allowing the tongue to loll out limply. The snake will give every appearance of being dead, but if you roll the Hog-Nose onto its belly, it will promptly flip itself onto its back again. It can stay in this sham-death position for hours if necessary, until the danger passes, whereupon the snake looks around, rolls back onto its belly, and goes on its way. Unfortunately, captive Hog-Noses soon learn that people are not a threat, and they give up their performance.

Hog-Nose snakes measure less than four feet long and can tolerate a wide range of environmental conditions. The one characteristic that removes them from consideration as a possible pet, however, is their very specialized food preference; most Hog-Nose snakes will not eat any food other than toads. Providing sufficient food for a Hog-Nose can be a daunting and frustrating task.

Southern Hog-Nose Snake.

Hog-Nose snakes also have enlarged rear fangs and a mild paralytic venom for subduing their prey. Although the venom is not dangerous to humans, this snake may nevertheless be classified in some jurisdictions as a venomous species.

Florida Water Snake.

8. Water Snakes *(Nerodia species)*

It is indeed a fortunate thing that water snakes rarely reach more than four or five feet in length, for they make one of the nastiest and most aggressive captives I

37

have ever seen. In the wild, water snakes are nervous
and defensive, and will quickly dart away at the least
disturbance. In captivity, where they cannot run away,
they instead turn on their keeper with unbelievable
ferocity, biting repeatedly and emptying the contents
of their anal glands while struggling to escape.

Having said that, it should be noted that some individual water snakes are quite calm and docile. In my
collection, I have a Banded Water Snake and a Broad-
Banded Water Snake that do not object to being held
even by young children. But even they can't resist an
occasional nip now and again.

9. Ringneck Snakes *(Diadophis punctatus)*

The beautiful little ringneck snake is a common inhabitant of the northeastern United States, where it can be
found in virtually any patch of forested woodland.
Although it is not a rare snake, it is seldom seen
because of its subterranean habits—it spends most of
its time prowling through underground burrows looking for earthworms.

*Southern
Ringneck
Snake.*

They can be occasionally found underneath rotting
logs or in wood piles, however, and it is the rare snake
fancier who can resist capturing such a handsome
snake and adding it to his collection. Ringnecks are
attractively colored, with a deep glossy blue or black
contrasting sharply with the bright yellow or red belly.

There is also a thin ring of yellow or red across the back of the neck. With the exception of the garter snakes, ringnecks are probably the most likely snake to be collected in the wild by most people.

They are, however, very delicate snakes, and do not do well in captivity. Since most captive ringnecks do not live more than a few months, it is best to leave them in the forests, where they can be enjoyed for years to come.

10. Racer Snakes *(Coluber constrictor)*

As the name suggests, these are very active snakes that require a lot of room. There are several varieties of racer snake, of which the Black Racer and the Blue Racer are the most common on dealers' lists. They are not large snakes, seldom exceeding four-and-a-half feet, and they require warm and dry environmental conditions.

Southern Black Racer.

Racer snakes, however, do not make very good captives. They are nervous and aggressive and never really settle down. Their defensiveness, combined with their speed, makes them very difficult to handle. Often, they will simply refuse to eat as long as they are confined. Even if they accept food, they are not likely to eat rodents, and must be provided with lizards or smaller snakes, which makes it difficult for the owner to obtain enough food for them.

Obtaining a Snake

Now that you've decided what kind of snake you'd like, the next step is finding somebody who has one to sell. There are three basic sources for pet snakes: local breeders or collectors, mail-order breeders or whole-salers, and local pet shops.

One of the best ways to obtain a pet snake is through a local breeder or collector. The advantages to this method are numerous. Most snake breeders are very conscientious about their animals and take extraordinary care in keeping and caring for them (if they didn't, they would have no litters of young snakes to sell). Since the breeder has a wealth of experience in keeping and raising this species, he will be able to answer any questions that you have, and

Professional breeders raise snakes for the pet-buying public.

can pass on useful information and tips on caring for your snake (I have met very few snake breeders who did not relish the chance to help out a beginner). Price-wise, most private breeders are competitive with mail-order dealers, without the shipping costs.

There are, however, a few disadvantages as well, and they must be carefully considered. The biggest problem in dealing with a local breeder is to find one. Unless you live in a large city, there are unlikely to be any snake breeders near you. Even if there were, since few local snake breeders advertise, the only way to find them is through word of mouth. Members of your local herpetological society should be able to point you to any reputable breeders in your area.

Another potential problem is variety. Breeding snakes takes a lot of room and some expenditure of money. For this reason, most private breeders tend to special-ize in one or at most a small number of species, and unless you are fortunate enough to find a person who breeds the species you are looking for, you may be out of luck.

The biggest problem, however, is that breeders prefer to sell their stock shortly after it is hatched; in fact, you may find that there is a waiting list of people who order snakes even before they are born.

For the most part, beginning snake keepers should avoid hatchling snakes. Although they are very brightly colored and many people find them absolutely adorable, hatchling snakes are very delicate and require constant attention. Because they are so small, they must be handled with exceptional care and can be easily injured. Also, they are very exacting in their environmental conditions, and require constant warmth and secure hiding spots.

Feeding them can also be a problem, since most hatchling snakes will only feed on newborn mice, or pinkies—and many hatchlings will not eat pinkies unless they are alive. Unless you can find a mouse breeder nearby, finding enough live newborn mice to feed your little snake will be a real problem. And you will need at least one pinkie a week to keep the snake happy and growing. It is also an unfortunate fact that some percentage of every litter of snakes will simply refuse to eat, and will calmly and deliberately starve themselves to death within a few months unless they are force-fed, and this is not a task for a beginning snake keeper.

ORDERING BY MAIL

By far the most versatile way to obtain a pet snake is through a mail-order dealer. For some of the more exotic snakes, moreover, this may be the only source. The addresses of several snake dealers are listed in the Resources section at the end of this book.

In general, you can expect to pay about half as much for a dealer's snake as you would in the pet store. On top of this price, however, you will need to pay the shipping costs (since it is illegal to send snakes through the mail, most dealers ship their snakes using air freight, and this runs between $35 and $45). Very often (especially if the weather is cool), you will also have to pay a box charge of $10 to $15 to cover the expenses of boxes, bags, heaters and shipping materials. Finally, most dealers have a minimum order requirement for anything they ship out, which can range from $50 to over $100. All of this may push the total cost of your snake pretty close to what you would pay in the pet store.

Check for anything unusual or suspicious on your snake or in its environment. This is a Two-headed Corn Snake.

The best way to place an order with a dealer is by telephone. The dealer will need to know what species you want and what airport you would like them shipped to (for an extra charge, you can sometimes have the air carrier itself deliver the package right to your door).

If there is a problem, you must contact the dealer at the earliest opportunity (within twenty-four hours). Only a very tiny proportion of shipped snakes do not survive the trip. If you are one of the unlucky ones, your dealer will probably request that you send him some verification of the snake's condition (most will accept a photograph of the dead snake resting on a current newspaper as sufficient proof). He will then ship you another snake.

ADVANTAGES OF THE PET STORE

One big advantage that a local pet store has over a mail-order dealer is that you will be able to closely examine any snakes that you are interested in before you buy them. The disadvantages are that you might pay more, and your selection will be limited to the species that the shop has available.

In many cases, it may be just as important to choose the right pet shop as it is to choose the right snake. Unless you are fortunate enough to find a pet shop that specializes in exotic animals, the smiling young woman at the pet store isn't likely to know any more about the particular needs of your species than you do.

Sadly, many pet stores tend to keep their reptiles in, shall we say, less than optimum conditions. This treatment is partly the result of financial considerations and lack of space, and is also due to a simple lack of knowledge about the needs of these animals. For this reason, it is imperative that you shop around, visiting as many pet stores as possible before you buy your snake.

Knowing What to Look For

Even an untrained eye can quickly pick out some danger signals that should steer you away from a particular store. Do the cages look clean and well-maintained, or do they have a dirty substrate, empty water dishes and no heat source? Do the animals look fed and alert, or are they sullen bags of skin and bone who are frantically trying to claw their way out? Do the animals have enough room to move around in their cages, or are they piled atop one another? Snakes that are kept in dirty, ill-maintained, overcrowded cages are much more likely to be stressed and to develop health problems later on. Avoid them.

If you are able to find a snake you want in a reputable pet store, take the opportunity to examine it carefully. Choosing a healthy snake to begin with will save you a lot of problems, heartache and expense down the road.

Signs of a Healthy Snake

A healthy and happy snake should be alert, and (if awake) will watch you carefully as you approach his cage. If the snake scrambles around frantically at your approach, chances are that it is not yet acclimated to captivity, and would not be a good choice to take home.

Always handle a snake before you buy it. (See chapter 6 for tips on how to handle a snake safely.) This not only allows you to judge how tame the snake is and

Snakes and
Their World

how well it tolerates handling, but it also gives you the opportunity to closely examine it for any potential health problems.

LOOK FOR MITES

The first things to look for are small moving dark dots between the scales, particularly around the eyes and lips. These are mites, and they are bad news. They are also highly contagious, so it is likely that if one snake in the store has them, the rest do, too.

CHECK THE NOSE AND MOUTH

The next things to check are the nose and mouth. If the snake is audibly wheezing while it breathes, or if it is breathing with its mouth open, or if you see a fluid bubbling or dripping from the nose, reject it

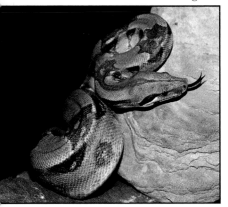

immediately. These are all signs of a respiratory infection, which is potentially life-threatening to the snake. A healthy snake only opens its mouth to drink or swallow food; even its tongue protrudes through a small slot in the upper lip, not the mouth itself.

Next, take a soft prod such as a pencil and gently pry open the snake's mouth (the snake will probably object quite vigorously

Pay particular attention to the scales at the tip of the snake's nose, which can be damaged by excessive rubbing. (Red-Tailed Boa)

to this, so make sure you have a firm grip and be careful not to break any of the snake's teeth). Carefully examine the inside of the mouth and throat for any sign of red, inflamed areas, an excess of watery fluid, or grey, cheesy matter. Any of these signals mean big trouble and big vet bills. A healthy snake's mouth should be smooth and free of any foreign matter.

CHECK THE SCALES

Carefully examine all of the snake's scales. If there are any patches where the scales are wrinkled or missing, this indicates a burn or scar injury. If the injury is

44

small, well-healed and doesn't seem to be causing the snake any difficulty, you might ignore it. Such old injuries are particularly common in snakes that have been fed live food. If the scarring is extensive, however, you probably want another snake.

Pay particular attention to the scales at the very tip of the snake's nose. If these look like they have been worn away or torn off, this is a sign that the snake has been rubbing his nose on the cage, looking for a way out. It may mean that the cage is too small, or that the snake hasn't been provided with a hiding box. Or it may mean that the snake has been wild-caught and hasn't yet adjusted to captivity.

NOTE OVERALL BEHAVIOR

While you are holding the snake, observe its general behavior and appearance. Individual snakes have different personalities, and one individual of a species may be a hissing, striking demon, while another will calmly glide around in your hands.

The snake should glide smoothly and steadily between your hands, with its tongue flickering to investigate you (you are, after all, just as new to the snake as it is to you). Snakes that are listless or that hang limply in your hands are probably suffering from some ailment. If the snake wraps around your arm while you are holding it (as most snakes will), the grip should feel firm and authoritative.

NOTE THE BODY

The snake's body should also look and feel solid. The skin should fit snugly, without any obvious folds or creases. If the outline of the snake's backbone is visible, or if there are longitudinal folds or creases in the skin, it means that the snake hasn't been eating, which may be a sign of further trouble. Since refusing to feed is a symptom of many health problems, make sure that the snake you want has been eating regularly and willingly.

45

Snakes and
Their World

Although any reputable store will offer you a health guarantee on your snake (usually seven days), this is in reality quite worthless. Any snake that is so ill that it will die within seven days will exhibit one or more of the signs above—a clear signal that you do not want it.

If the snake is in the initial or early stages of an illness, the signs may not be noticeable when you buy it, but in that case, it will take the snake much longer than seven days to show symptoms or die from the ailment.

A healthy snake's body should be lithe and strong. (Madagascar Ringed Snake)

Quarantine the New Snake

Because it may take several weeks for the signs of an illness to be visible, it is a good idea to quarantine any new snake that you bring home, particularly if you already have other snakes or reptiles. Quarantining is simply the process of isolating any new snake for a period of time, so that any potential health problems can be seen and treated before the rest of your collection is exposed to it. Even if this will be your first snake, you should not skip the quarantine—it is necessary in order to watch for signs of any impending illness.

The quarantine tank should be designed for spartan functionality rather than attractiveness. A 10- or 20-gallon aquarium (depending on the size of the snake) with a locking screen lid, a newspaper substrate, a cardboard hide box, a water dish and a heating lamp will do. The quarantine tank should be in an entirely separate room from the rest of your collection.

Whenever you service your snake cages, for feeding, cleaning or other tasks, you should always service the quarantine tank last, to avoid carrying pathogens or parasites from one cage to the next. It may also be helpful to keep the temperature in the quarantine tank a few degrees higher than normal.

Choosing
a Snake

WATCH YOUR NEWCOMER

Keep a close eye on your new snake for a period of at least thirty days, keeping in mind all of the potential danger signals mentioned above. You should also examine the snakes feces whenever they appear—and this is where the newspaper substrate shows its superiority in the quarantine tank.

If the feces are loose or watery, if they begin to develop a greenish color, or if they begin to take on a strong unpleasant odor, this may indicate the beginning of intestinal troubles. Also, if the feces contain a number of thin objects that look like pieces of thread, be aware that these are worms, and they will need to be eliminated by a veterinarian (see chapter 7).

Most snakes that are sick will usually begin to show symptoms within thirty to forty-five days. Some snake keepers, particularly those with large collections, like to keep their new arrivals quarantined for at least sixty days (once a disease or parasite has been introduced into a large collection, it is very difficult to contain and control).

If, at the end of the quarantine period, your snake is still healthy and feeding regularly, you can move it into its regular cage. After removing the snake, the entire quarantine cage and all of its contents should be emptied and cleaned with a strong salt-water solution or a disinfectant (do *not* use any cleanser containing pine oil or pine tar—they are very toxic to snakes), followed by a thorough rinsing with lots of water. After replacing the hide box and the newspaper flooring, the quarantine tank is ready for the next arrival.

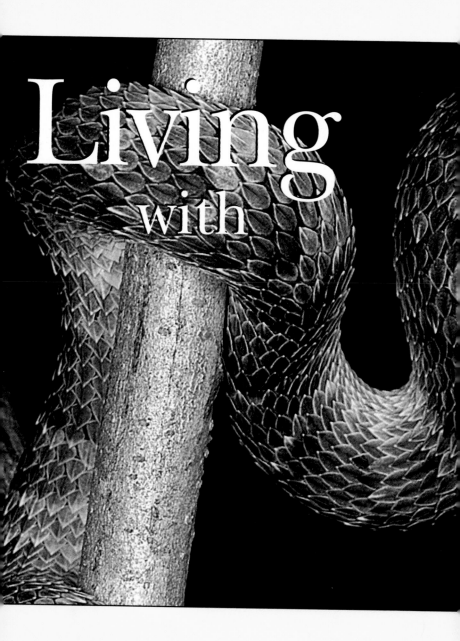

Living
with

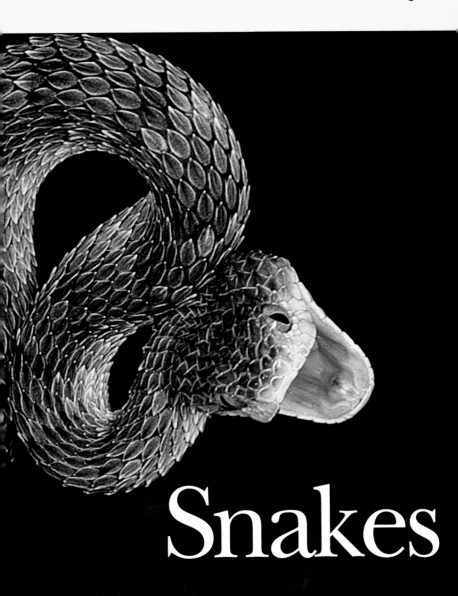

part two

Snakes

chapter 4

Housing
Your **Snake**

For the vast majority of snakes, the most practical and least expensive accommodation is an ordinary tropical fish aquarium. Any pet shop will have a number of different aquariums in several different shapes and sizes, and at very inexpensive prices.

What Size Tank?

The size tank you will need depends on the size of your snake. Most snakes are not very active, and spend most of their time curled up in a corner or inside their hide box. Therefore, a pet snake can get by with a surprisingly small cage. Small snakes, such as garters or green snakes, will have plenty of room in a standard 10-gallon aquarium. Medium-sized snakes, such as corns, kings or young boids, can get by with a 10-gallon, but would do much better in a 20-gallon tank. Active snakes such as racers or bull snakes will require the larger size tank.

Larger boids will need at least a 55-gallon tank, but eventually they will outgrow even that, and will require a custom-built cage. As a general rule of thumb, a snake's cage should be about two-thirds as long as the snake, and about half as wide as the snake's length. A bigger tank never hurts, however, and will come in handy if you decide to expand your snake collection.

Very often, people who buy their snakes in a pet store will notice that most pet shops keep all their

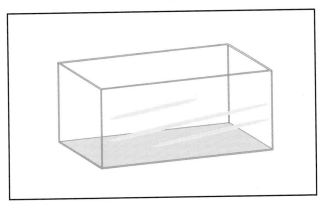

Small snakes are fine in a 10-gallon tank, but larger snakes will need the 20-gallon (or larger) size.

snakes—even such large ones as baby boids—crowded into small 10-gallon aquariums. Do not duplicate this at home, as this is simply a way for the pet store to save some space. Pet store snakes are usually not kept in such cramped and crowded quarters long enough to do them much harm, since they are sold right away.

Many people also seem to have the idea that a snake's size and growth can be limited if it is kept in a smaller tank, or that a snake will not grow larger than its cage will allow. *This is not true.* Snakes, like all reptiles, grow continuously through life. Keeping your snake in a smaller tank will not limit his growth, but will only make him cramped and unhealthy. For this reason, it is best to provide a large enough cage for your snake to grow into.

The Tank's Shape

The shape of the tank can also be just as important as the size. For snakes that spend most of their time on the ground, such as king snakes, garters or milk snakes, the tank does not need to be tall, but should have as much surface area at the bottom as possible. Twenty-gallon aquariums, for instance, come in a high style and a low. Both have the same volume, but the high tank is much taller, with a smaller bottom area than the low model of the same size. If your snake is a bottom-dweller and doesn't climb very much, the low style of tank is preferable.

Snakes that spend most of their time on the ground will prefer a longer tank, whereas climbing snakes will prefer taller tanks.
(Sunglow Phase Albino Corn Snake)

If your snake species is partly arboreal and likes to climb (for example, corn and rat snakes, or baby boids), you will need to provide enough vertical space to include a tree branch for climbing. In this case, the "high" style of tank is the best.

The Lid

No matter what size or shape tank you select, you will also need a securely locking lid. The plastic hoods with fluorescent lighting that are available for tropical fish aquariums are not suitable for keeping snakes, since they offer an easy avenue of escape. The solution usually adopted by small boys who have captured a frog or snake—placing a window screen over the tank and piling some bricks or books atop it—simply will not work.

Snakes are superb escape artists, and if there is any way at all out of their cages, they will eventually find it. And if the snake can get the tip of its nose under one corner of the screen, it will be able to wedge the rest of its body through and escape. Since snakes are surprisingly strong, and since in any case they do not need to lift the whole lid—just one corner of it—that pile of bricks or books will not keep a determined snake in its cage.

Even if the snake seems to be too small to reach the top of its tank, most species will be able to wedge their bodies into a corner, and, by pressing against the two edges, work their way up and out. Every snake cage, therefore, must be provided with a tightly fitting lid that can be securely locked into place.

You will need a very secure lid for your snake's tank. This is an aluminum frame screen, commonly available for aquariums.

SCREENED LIDS

Fortunately, most pet stores and many reptile supply houses sell pre-manufactured screened lids, which are of the correct dimensions needed to fit the standard aquarium sizes. These come in three basic types. The first, usually with an aluminum frame and wire mesh, fits over the top of the aquarium frame and uses special metal hinges and clips that fasten it securely to the plastic lip that runs along the outside edge of most aquariums. (Usually, the metal clips and hinges must be bought separately.) These lids fit very securely; if necessary, extra clips and hinges can be added for more strength.

One disadvantage of this type of lid, however, is that the wire mesh tends to be rather open, and is often wide enough for a snake to push its nose through the holes and rub its scales raw on the wire.

Plastic or Metal Lids

The second type of lid is usually made from black plastic or metal and fits inside the tank, lying atop the narrow rim which runs around the inside lip of most aquariums. The lid is secured by turning two knobs at either end, which hook a little latch underneath the lip of the tank and prevent the lid from being lifted off.

Instead of using wire mesh, this type of lid has a large number of tiny holes punched through its surface for ventilation, which helps to prevent injuries caused by the snake rubbing its nose against the screen. It is usually less expensive as well.

One major disadvantage, however, is that there are no clips to secure the middle of the lid on the long sides— and the lid material itself is usually flexible enough to allow a determined snake to lift the edge, pry its nose through and escape.

The Railed Lid

The third type of lid is undoubtedly the best, but also the most difficult to procure. In this setup, the tank itself is modified, and has a narrow rail that runs along the edges of the rim. The screen lid slides into this rail from the front, somewhat like a sliding glass door. Once the lid is in place, it can be locked by placing a small peg through a hole at the front of the lid.

This type of lid is undoubtedly the most secure and, if pegged, is virtually escape-proof. However, this type of lid requires the use of a modified aquarium, too, and this combination tends to cost more than an ordinary aquarium and a screen lid. Also, you are not likely to see this type of tank for sale in a local pet store, and will probably have to order it from a reptile or tropical fish supply dealer.

Tank Substrate

There are a wide variety of materials that can be used as the substrate for a snake cage.

Newspaper The most functional and least expensive lining is ordinary newspaper. This can be cut to size and placed in the cage (three or four layers thick), and can be quickly and easily cleaned when necessary simply by removing the old layers, throwing them away and replacing them with fresh sheets.

Because newspaper is fairly absorbent and snake droppings do not contain much moisture, it is unlikely that there will be any problem with wastes soaking through to the cage floor. A newspaper substrate also makes it easy to spot ticks, mites and other parasites, as well as changes in the snake's feces. For this reason, all quarantine tanks should use newspaper as a substrate.

This Broad-Banded Water Snake lives on a soil and sphagnum moss substrate.

The disadvantage to a cage lined with newspaper, of course, is that it looks ugly and unnatural. If you don't mind the rather sterile appearance of such a cage, then newspaper substrate is plentiful, easily obtained and costs next to nothing. If, on the other hand, you would like a more natural appearance for your snake's cage (it makes no difference whatever to the snake), then you will need to use some other substrate.

Pine/Cedar Shavings One substrate to definitely *avoid* is pine or cedar shavings, such as those used to keep mice or hamsters. The small particles of dust that

55

are produced by these shavings are very irritating to a snake's lungs and mouth, and the volatile oils that are present (particularly in cedar) can be very toxic to snakes.

Not only should one never keep a snake of any type on cedar shavings, but one should never feed a snake any rodent that has been kept on cedar shavings. The toxic oil may still be clinging to the mouse's fur and could poison your snake.

Soil or Sand   Natural tanks, which use a layer of soil with live plants as a substrate, should also be avoided. Not only are they difficult to clean and maintain, but snakes will tend to dig into the substrate and uproot the plants, quickly destroying the setup.

Shredded Bark   One quite usable substrate is made up of shredded tree bark or some other natural material. Among the substances offered for sale are orchid bark, aspen wood chips (*not* wood shavings), cocoa bean shells and ground-up corn cobs. I have also seen keepers use ordinary rabbit pellets as a substrate, and many hobbyists line their cages with dried natural sphagnum moss. These materials are relatively inexpensive to use, and are absorbent and easy to clean—simply scoop out the feces and replace a handful of the substrate. (This doesn't work with moss, however—here, you have to replace the entire substrate rather often.) They also retain heat well and show off the snake's colors to good advantage.

One disadvantage of this type of substrate, however, is that if you are feeding your snake such slimy prey as frogs or worms, the pieces of bedding material will stick to it and be swallowed by the snake, where they can cause serious problems. Another disadvantage is that most of these materials tend to get moldy and begin to rot if they get wet, either from the snake's droppings or from water splashed from the snake's dish. These substrates must therefore be cleaned nearly every day, and the soiled spots replaced with a bit of fresh material.

GRAVEL

Most of the pre-packaged snake kits that you find in a pet shop use ordinary aquarium gravel as a substrate. Although gravel is a workable substrate (I have raised several dozen snakes on gravel), it has lately fallen out of favor with most snake keepers because of the danger that it can be swallowed by the snake and pass on to the intestines, where it can cause severe blockages. Usually, however, this is not a problem in snakes that are being fed rodents—although it can be a danger to those that eat such slimy and sticky food as frogs, fish or worms.

If the gravel is pea-sized or larger, it is unlikely that it will be swallowed by a rodent eater. Gravel, however, is not absorbent and can be difficult to keep clean unless it is either replaced often or is periodically removed, rinsed and dried.

ASTROTURF

The most popular, and in many ways the best, substrate is a sheet of green artificial plastic material, known somewhat jokingly as Astroturf. This material comes in single sheets that are presized to fit inside most standard aquariums, where it lies on the bottom like a carpet.

Although Astroturf is attractive, relatively inexpensive (and by the way, the turf sold in hardware or garden stores is the same as that in pet shops, and costs a lot less) and easy to use, it has two disadvantages. Since the edges are usually rough-cut, there are small plastic strings which continually unravel from the edges, and these can present severe problems if they are accidentally swallowed by your snake.

One solution to this problem is to buy a sheet of Astroturf that is slightly larger than the bottom of the tank, and then, using a needle and fishing line, fold the edges under and sew them shut like a hem. This prevents the strings of plastic from wearing off.

Another problem with Astroturf is that, being plastic, it is not absorbent and must be cleaned frequently, and this entails dismantling all of the cage furnishings and removing the liner. Most snake keepers who use Astroturf will have two sheets, so they can place one sheet in the tank while the other is being cleaned.

The Snake's Hide Box

Because snakes are prey animals as well as predators, and are often attacked and eaten by other animals (among the animals that will eat snakes are hawks, eagles, raccoons, pigs and skunks), they spend most of their time safely hidden in a nook or cranny such as a burrow or a tree hollow. They particularly dislike being exposed, since this makes them vulnerable to birds of prey, against which they have virtually no effective defense. For this reason, snakes need to feel physically secure and safe before they will engage in any other activities, including eating.

In the wild, snakes are sure to travel along routes that include hiding places. In captivity, your snake will need these same opportunities.

In captivity, snakes must get this feeling of security from a hide box. This is simply any sort of dark, closed-in retreat where the snake can curl up and feel protected. Commercial hide boxes are available that look like natural rocks but are of molded plastic. Some are electrically heated, but this is not really necessary.

A usable hide box can also be constructed inside the tank using flat rocks to make a sort of cave. In a pinch, an ordinary shoe box with a small hole cut in one side can serve as a temporary retreat.

A hide box need not be very large. To feel secure, the snake will prefer a small, closed-in area, where it can coil up with its body touching all sides of the box. A box measuring just 8 × 10 × 3 inches is big enough to serve as a hiding spot for a typical five- or six-foot snake. The entrance hole should be just big enough for the snake to squeeze through.

Some arboreal snakes, such as young Ball pythons, prefer to have their hide boxes located off the ground. This can be accomplished by attaching a small wooden box to the Y of a large tree branch.

Heat is a snake's fuel, since the higher the temperature the faster it digests food and performs other biological functions. (Striped/ Speckled King Snake)

Heat

Because snakes, like all reptiles, are ectotherms and cannot produce their own body heat, they must be provided with sufficient outside heat sources to maintain their optimum body temperatures. Temperature is the single most crucial factor in successfully keeping snakes in captivity—nearly every potential health problem snakes face can be directly traced to how well their thermal requirements are being met.

In a sense, heat can be thought of as the snake's fuel— the higher the temperature, the faster the snake's metabolism becomes, the more quickly it can move, and the more easily it can digest food, resist disease and perform other biological functions.

How Hot?

No single temperature is best for keeping snakes. Snakes from differing ecological zones will require different ranges of temperature. Temperate snakes such as garters and rat snakes do well in temperatures between 75 and 80 degrees, while tropical or desert species such as boids or bull snakes need higher temperatures. As a rough average, most snakes will do well at daytime temperatures averaging in the low 80s, dropping at night to the mid-70s, with a daytime basking spot of around 90.

In addition, the specific temperature requirements for any snake will vary from day to day and perhaps moment to moment, depending upon what biological activity the snake is engaged in. Digestion of food, for instance, often requires higher temperatures than does capturing food.

Thermoregulation

Since it is not possible for the snake keeper to know precisely what temperature is needed by the snake at any given moment, the solution is to provide a range of different temperatures, or a "temperature gradient," and allow the snake to select the temperature that it wants, by moving from warmer to cooler areas as needed. This process is known as "thermoregulation."

No Hot Rocks

The electric "hot rocks" or "sizzle stones" which are often sold in pet stores should not be used in any snake's cage. The cheaper ones usually do not give you any means of controlling the heat output and thus no way to regulate the temperature. The more expensive ones may have a rheostat which allows manual heat control, but there are other problems.

Most heat rocks are prone to malfunctions, and will often overheat until they melt their wiring, presenting serious risk of burns to the snake. Also, the heat rocks do not warm the surrounding air very much, and the only way for the snake to obtain the heat is through physical contact with the heater.

Since snakes have few nerve endings in their bellies, it is not at all rare for them to sit unknowingly on an overheated hot rock, unaware that their skin is being severely burned. Because they only heat one small spot in the tank, sizzle stones are also useless in providing a workable temperature gradient, and do not help the snake to thermoregulate effectively.

Finally, hot rocks do not allow the snakes to mimic their natural behavior patterns, since the majority of snakes obtain most of their heat by basking in strong sunlight, rather than by contact with a heated surface. Most snakes prefer that their heat source come from above.

It may seem to be a simple matter to place the snake's cage near a window, where it will receive warmth from direct sunlight. An enclosed aquarium in direct sunlight, however, would quickly trap the heat and raise the temperature to lethal levels.

BASKING LAMPS

For years, most snake keepers have duplicated the warming effects of the sun by using incandescent basking lamps in their cages, and in most cases, this is still the best option.

Unlike some other reptiles, snakes do not need any exposure to natural sunlight or ultraviolet wavelengths, and they do not require full-spectrum lighting in their cages. In fact, snakes that are exposed to ultraviolet light tend to become unnaturally darker.

For this reason, a snake's basking spot can be set up using an ordinary incandescent light bulb with a reflector. It should be mounted on the outside of the cage at one corner of the screen lid, to insure that the snake cannot physically touch the light bulb, since inadvertent contact could cause severe burns.

A flat pile of rocks—or, for arboreal species, a heavy tree branch—should be arranged directly below the

Living with
Snakes

basking spot. In this way, the light will produce a localized "hot spot" for basking while leaving the far end of the tank relatively unheated, producing a temperature gradient for the snake to use in thermoregulation.

It is usually best to place a hide box at each end of the tank, allowing the snake to choose a warm or cool resting spot. If there is room for only one hide box, place it at the far end of the tank.

The size, power and distance of the light bulb must be determined through trial and error. The determination of these variables will depend upon the temperature range desired as well as the size and dimensions of the tank. For most snakes, the temperature directly under the basking light should be in the 95 to 100 degrees range, while the temperature at the far end should be around 75 degrees. Tropical snakes need basking spots of 100 to 105 degrees and cool spots in the low 80s. In most tanks, a 75- or 100-watt light bulb will provide adequate heat.

TIMING THE LIGHT

For best results, the basking light should be connected to an electrical timer to turn it on and off automatically. Most tropical snakes prefer a 12-hour on, 12-hour off schedule, which mimics the length of the tropical day. Temperate-zone snakes will also do well with a tropical light schedule; however, if you plan to breed the snake, it is best to mimic the natural length of the day, making the photoperiod shorter in winter and longer in summer.

TANK CONSIDERATIONS

To properly house your snake, you'll need to pay attention to these factors when choosing your tank: size, shape, security and stuff.

Size: The tank should be large enough for the snake to move around, but since snakes aren't very active, they don't need too much room. A good rule of thumb is that the cage be about two-thirds as long as the snake and about half as wide as the snake is long. For small snakes, a 10-gallon tank is fine. Larger snakes will need 20-gallon, 55-gallon or larger sizes.

Shape: If you have a snake that spends most of its time on the ground, you'll need a tank that's longer than it is high. If your snake is an arboreal species, your tank should be high enough for a climbing branch.

Security: Snakes are escape artists, so it's crucial that your tank have a securely fitting, escape-proof lid.

Stuff: To stimulate and satisfy your snake in its environment, you'll need some "stuff" for its tank. This includes proper substrate material, a hide box, a climbing branch, vegetation (real or artificial) and a shallow water dish.

CERAMIC HEATERS

Recently, a new heating device has been introduced to snake hobbyists, and it has replaced incandescent basking lights in many collections. This innovation is the ceramic heating element, which uses a heat bulb and a socket that looks somewhat like a light bulb, but which gives off only heat, not light.

Ceramic elements can be connected to small thermostats for very precise heat control—which unfortunately also makes them much more expensive than ordinary basking lights.

One problem with the ceramic heating elements, however, is that they do not produce any visible light, and all snakes need a photoperiod and a light/dark cycle. A light cycle can be provided by connecting an ordinary fluorescent lamp to the cage alongside the heater; but for the most part, the ceramic elements are better suited to lizard cages, where additional full-spectrum lighting is a necessity anyway. For most snake cages, it is much simpler and much less expensive to use an incandescent basking light to provide both light and heat.

WARMTH FROM BELOW

A few snakes, including desert-adapted snakes such as bull snakes and the heavy-bodied boids, will do best if, in addition to a radiant heat source from above, they have an artificially warmed substrate from which to get belly heat, which aids in digestion. Electric hot rocks and heated plastic hide boxes are intended to perform this function, but as we have seen, they are best avoided.

There are two other sources of bottom heat. The first is the undertank heater, which is constructed like a tiny heating pad or electric blanket. They are placed underneath the snake cage, where they produce heat which diffuses through the floor of the tank and substrate.

The heat tape is similar, but takes the form of a long electric ribbon which fastens to the bottom of the tank. Both produce enough heat to penetrate half-inch plywood and produce temperatures in the low 80s. Both are, however, also rather expensive. Fortunately, they are not really needed for most snakes.

THERMOMETER

It should go without saying that every snake cage should contain at least one thermometer to allow the temperature to be monitored. The stick-on thermometers used in tropical fish tanks work well and are inexpensive. Some snake keepers like to have two thermometers, one at the warm end and one at the cool end of the tank.

Your snake will need a climbing branch of suitable size and wood type. (Red-Tailed Boa)

Cage Furniture

Most snakes will do quite well in a tank consisting of substrate, a water dish, a hide box and a heat lamp. Such cages are rather unattractive, however, and most owners will want to include some sort of decoration or furniture for the snake tank.

With the exception of a climbing branch, which will be used by arboreal or partly arboreal species, these decorations are of no use at all for the snake—they are there solely for the pleasure of the snake keeper.

CLIMBING BRANCHES

Climbing branches should be strong and sturdy enough to support the weight of the snake without breaking, and long enough to provide ample climbing space. Although pet stores usually sell plastic tree branches, the real thing is also suitable, provided it is properly disinfected—and, of course, it can also be had for free. (Note that pine, spruce and other resinous trees are not suitable for use in a snake cage.)

ROCK PILES

Many snake keepers like to place a small, flat pile of rocks in their cages, which not only helps retain heat from the basking light, but also provides the snake with a rough surface upon which to shed its skin.

Rocks, tree branches, bark and other such furnishings must be carefully cleaned and disinfected before they are placed in your cage, since they may harbor parasites such as mites and ticks. The best way to disinfect them is to soak them overnight in a 3 percent solution of sodium hypochlorite (ordinary laundry bleach) or a strong salt solution. This should be enough to kill any nasties that may be hiding within. Afterwards, the object must be thoroughly washed in a large amount of water to rinse away any trace of the disinfectant. (Please note that commercial disinfectants that contain pine tar or pine oil are *extremely* toxic to most reptiles, and should *never* be used to clean a reptile's cage or anything in it.)

PLANTS (LIVE AND ARTIFICIAL)

Some hobbyists also like to keep live plants in their snake cage, to give it a more natural appearance. This will not harm the snake, but it is certainly possible for the snake to harm the plant by crawling over it and crushing it.

For ease in cleaning and to prevent the plant from being repeatedly uprooted, all terrarium plants should be placed in a pot, and this should be buried in the substrate up to the rim. Any selected plants should be strong and capable of taking the weight of the snake without breaking. Remember that live plants will have to be watered every day. Of course, it is also possible to

*You can use
real or artificial
plants in your
snake cage.
(Corn Snake)*

use artificial plants, which always look good and never need to be cared for.

Humidity

For most snakes, the humidity level found in the average home (about 55 percent) will be acceptable, and no changes need be made. (But some homes may become too dry in wintertime and may require increased humidity in the snake's cage.) For several species of snakes, however, including the boids, humidity levels are important for maintaining the health of the snake.

One of the most common problems in captive boids is incomplete shedding of the skin, which is nearly always caused by a humidity level that is too low. Ball pythons and Rainbow boas in particular require quite high humidity levels, especially when they are about to shed.

One sure sign that the humidity level is too low is the appearance of "dents" or "dimples" in the clear scale covering the snake's eyes.

High humidity should *not* be maintained by closing off the screen lid, as this will cut off the circulation of air within the tank.

WATER PANS

The best way to maintain a high humidity is to place a large water pan inside the tank. For many boids, which like to soak for long periods at a time, this is necessary anyway. Plastic water bowls that are molded to look like natural rock are available in pet shops, and come in various sizes and shapes; however, any shallow bowl that is big enough for the snake to curl up inside, and heavy enough not to be tipped over, will serve.

Another technique which works well for boids is to line the snake's hide box with damp moss or a damp towel. This can produce humidity levels as high as 90 percent, and virtually guarantees a complete shed. It also allows the snake to move from higher to lower humidity areas as it wishes. The moss or towel will have to be dampened again periodically as it dries out.

Hibernation

As we have already seen, one of the most important factors in any snake's life is maintaining the proper body temperature. In temperate areas during winter, daylight hours grow so short, and the temperatures drop so low, that the snake is unable to maintain its preferred body temperature. As a result, it is forced to stop feeding and retreat to an underground den, where its body temperature may drop as low as 40 degrees. Enzymatic action and bodily activities come to a virtual standstill, and the snake maintains this state

Any shallow bowl big enough for the snake to curl up in and heavy enough not to tip over will serve. (Eastern Garter Snake)

of hibernation (more correctly, the snake undergoes brumation, but the term hibernation is more common and will be used here) until warmer temperatures and longer days arrive in the spring.

Hibernation is, however, a very stressful and dangerous time for a snake. A considerable proportion of snakes will die during their hibernation period. Fortunately for the snake hobbyist, most species of snake do not require hibernation unless it is intended to breed them—the male snake manufactures and stores sperm during the low-temperature periods of hibernation, and cannot successfully breed in the spring unless he undergoes a period of hibernation first.

As long as your snake is kept at normal temperatures throughout the winter, it will usually remain active and continue to feed (although it may eat less in the winter than it does the rest of the year). If you don't intend to breed your snake, and thus hibernation is not critical, it is better not to attempt it at all.

HEAT AND LIGHT

Because snakes are ectotherms, meaning they depend on the environment to raise their body temperature sufficiently to digest food and perform other body functions, proper heat and light are necessary for their survival.

Snakes from different ecological zones will have different temperature requirements, and even those will change depending on what biological activity the snake needs to perform. Therefore, captive snakes need temperature gradients—places where it's warm and places where it's cool—in the tank. Basking lamps and hide boxes provide this variation. As for the amount of light and the amount of darkness needed in a day, most tropical areas have a "12 and 12" night/day ratio, and this is a good schedule for most captive snakes.

Some snakes, however, including the pine and bull snakes, seem to be genetically programmed to hibernate regardless of the weather, and may become inactive even if they are kept artificially warm. In these circumstances, it becomes very dangerous to maintain normal temperatures, since the snake will refuse to eat even though its metabolic rate remains high, and it will very likely use up its fat reserves and starve before beginning to accept food again in the spring.

If your snake refuses to eat at all during the winter and spends most of its time curled up inactively in its hide box, you will probably have to allow it to hibernate.

To prepare the snake for hibernation, gradually reduce the temperature in the cage by a few degrees per day until it is about 50 degrees. At this point, the snake will be torpid and unmoving. Gently place the snake in a hide box that has been packed with slightly damp moss or towels and place it in a basement, porch, or other area with a temperature between 45 and 50 degrees (some snake keepers have successfully hibernated snakes by placing them in the refrigerator). Leave the snake there for a period of at least ten weeks, checking in every few days to make sure that everything is all right.

At the end of the hibernation period, reverse this process by raising the temperature in the tank until it reaches normal levels. If all goes well, your snake should be ready to eat again within a few days of reaching optimum temperature.

If Your Snake Escapes

No matter how well-built your snake cage is, if you keep snakes for any length of time, sooner or later you will have an escape. Snakes are consummate escape artists—they make Houdini look like a rank amateur— and if there is any possible way out of confinement, they will eventually find it. They are also quick to take advantage of the slightest momentary lapse of judgement on the part of their keeper. A lid left unclipped, a door left slightly ajar, and your snake may turn up missing.

All may not be lost. If the snake has not been missing for very long, chances are it has not gone far. More than likely, it has found a comfortable spot somewhere in the room to curl up for a while. Since most snakes are active at night, however, it is likely that you will not notice the escape until morning. By that time, the snake could be anywhere.

A couple of things might help you track down your missing snake. Snakes do not like to be in open areas, since this exposes them to predators. Snakes loose in a room, therefore, tend to stick to the edges of the room and move along the walls. Pipes, holes in the wall and spaces under doorways are irresistible temptations, as are heating ducts and ventilation screens, and it does not take a very big hole to admit a snake. If you can fit your index finger through a hole, a snake can probably fit his body through it.

As morning comes, after having wandered and explored all night, the snake will look for a "hide box" in which to spend the day. This will have all of the characteristics of the hide box in its cage—it will be warm, dark and confined. Among the spaces to check for a missing snake are closets, inside shoes or boots, underneath furniture (the back of a refrigerator is a favored spot), inside clothing piles and between books or bookshelves.

Also, remember to look up as well. Some snakes, particularly rat snakes and young boids, are very good climbers, and can easily ascend what would seem to be an impossible climb. Look for them perched atop refrigerators and bookshelves, the top shelves of closets, and lying along the tops of curtain rods and drapes.

HOUSING CHECKLIST

Here, in summary, is a list of all you will need to provide your snake with a secure home. (All of these supplies together should cost less than $100.)

20-gallon aquarium

12 x 30-inch galvanized metal screen cover

Screen top hinges

Screen top clips

Astroturf cage lining

Incandescent 75-watt basking light

Simulated rock water bowl, medium size

Simulated rock hide box

Stick-on thermometer

Sometimes the snake can be incredibly clever in selecting a hiding spot. Once, while I was cleaning out my reptile room, I unthinkingly left the door slightly ajar for less than a minute. My five-foot bull snake seized the opportunity and made a break for it. After I noticed she was missing, I searched the adjacent rooms for over two hours, finally finding her in the bathroom, calmly curled up inside the toilet, underneath the rim.

It may take a few days to find your snake. One trick to use is to sprinkle a small amount of flour along the edge of the floor near the walls. If the snake passes by, he will leave a tell-tale trail. Another trick that I have seen used is to place a food item such as a mouse in a wire cage which has a mesh just wide enough to admit the snake. Many times, the snake will enter the cage, swallow the mouse and then be too fat to exit the way he came. You will find him sitting forlornly in the cage in the morning.

If the snake has managed to find its way outside through a window screen or open door, it is unlikely that you will ever see it again. (You may, however, get lucky—after one of my red rat snakes was accidentally let out of his room by a friend, I searched the house for two weeks and finally gave up. Several weeks later, my neighbor's daughter found Callisto happily sunning himself in her backyard garden.)

chapter 5

Feeding

Your **Snake**

One of the most diffi-
cult aspects of snake
keeping for most peo-
ple is the business of
feeding. All snakes are
carnivorous and need
animal prey. While
other popular pets,
such as dogs and cats,
are also carnivores and
eat animal prey, their

commercially available food has been processed and packaged so
much that it is scarcely recognizable as the flesh of dead animals.

Cute Food

Snakes, by contrast, must have their food in a natural and
unprocessed state, which is far more upsetting to most people—
particularly since the preferred food of most snakes, mice and other
rodents, consists of species which some people themselves keep as

pets, and which most people view as being "cute." Moreover, the snake's preferred method of killing their intended food is one which many people view as "cruel"—even though it is the quickest and most effective way for a limbless animal to procure food. While it would be much nicer (and easier) if snakes would eat pizza and french fries, they do not, and any beginning snake keeper must quickly come to terms with the dietary requirements of his or her pet.

Swallowing your prey head first makes it go down a little easier.

The Mouse Diet

Although snakes as a group will prey on a large variety of food animals, ranging from rodents to birds to frogs to other snakes, nearly all captive snakes will live happily on a diet of whole mice. Whole mice, which includes the viscera and stomach contents, are a nutritionally complete diet for all snakes that will eat them. No vitamin supplements or dietary additions are needed.

Some snakes will accept other readily available foods, such as earthworms or fish, and these are also acceptable diets if they consist of fresh, whole animals, with bones and viscera included.

Larger Prey

The large boids present some feeding problems that other species do not. A big boa or python will turn up its nose at a mere mouse. It requires food of at least rat size, and may even need larger prey such as rabbits or chickens. It would seem logical to choose a different prey species for the boid as it grows, beginning with mice for a hatchling, rats for a medium-sized specimen, and finally graduating to larger rabbits or chickens.

This sounds good in theory and may even work, but unfortunately, boids can be incredibly picky and stubborn when it comes to food preferences. Once they have become accustomed to a particular food animal, they may stubbornly resist any change in diet, which can become a real problem when you have a ten-foot python that refuses to eat anything but rats—six or seven of them at a time.

Stick to One Species

One way to avoid this problem is to feed the snake a single species of prey animal throughout its entire life. Baby boids get baby rats, bunnies or chicks, with the size of the prey increasing as the snake grows. (Most boids won't object to an occasional temporary switch to a different prey item, but a prolonged switch may not be tolerated.)

Ball Pythons in particular can be incredibly finicky about their food, and have a disconcerting habit of suddenly refusing to eat for long periods of time. In many cases, this is due to some incorrect environmental factor (usually a temperature that is too low), but in some cases it is because the snake itself has suddenly developed an objection to the type of food it is being fed.

For example, a Ball Python that has eaten white rats uncomplainingly for months may suddenly refuse to eat white rats at all, but will gulp down black ones. It may also decide that it wants birds instead of rats. Such finicky eating habits can be an unending source of frustration, and are one reason why Ball Pythons can be rather difficult to care for. (Other species can also occasionally exhibit the same stubbornness; I once had a Texas Rat Snake yearling that refused to eat anything except tree frogs, and then only grey ones, not green. Needless to say, I did not keep this snake for very long.)

Large Amounts of Food Aren't Necessary

Because snakes are ectotherms and do not produce their own body heat, they do not need large amounts of food to devote to maintaining their metabolism. Consequently, a typical snake can get by on less than one-fifth the amount of food that would be required by a similarly sized mammal. Also, a snake's digestive system is much more efficient than a mammal's, insuring that the snake gets more food value per unit of food.

For these reasons, snakes do not require a large amount of food to be kept happy and healthy. Most medium-sized rodent eaters, such as corn snakes and king snakes, will grow steadily on a diet of one properly sized mouse every two weeks. (A "properly sized" food animal is one that is slightly larger than the widest girth of the snake.)

Larger snakes may require larger food animals, such as rats, and large boids may need to be fed chickens or rabbits, but they are also capable of thriving on one meal every two or three weeks. Snakes that consume cold-blooded prey such as fish or earthworms may need to be fed a bit more often, say, once every six or seven days. And any snake, if fed an exceptionally large meal, may be able to go for a month or two before it needs to eat again.

Live or Pre-killed Food?

There is a very common misperception among people, even among many snake hobbyists, that snakes must have live prey. This is not usually true. In the wild, snakes, like most other carnivores, will usually take any opportunity to get a free and easy meal, and will not pass up a freshly killed prey animal if they happen upon it. In fact, snakes have been known to eat a fair amount of carrion that has been dead for some time, and the stomachs of wild snakes often contain prey that must have been in an advanced state of decomposition when it was eaten.

Although your snake may prefer to eat live prey, which it kills itself through constriction, this is not at all necessary for the health of the snake. In fact, it is best *not* to feed your captive snakes live prey at all.

Some snakes, such as garter snakes, water snakes and green snakes, eat prey animals such as fish, earthworms, insects or frogs, which are defenseless and cannot cause any damage to the snake. In these cases, the snakes do not even bother to kill their prey before they eat it; they simply seize it in the jaws and proceed to swallow it alive. Rodent eaters, however, are dealing with prey that is potentially lethal, and they must kill their food before they can swallow it.

Most snakes kept as pets are constrictors. In this method of killing prey, the snake will seize the animal in its jaws and very quickly wrap its body into a series of coils which envelop the prey, squeezing it with powerful muscles. Contrary to what

HELP!! MY SNAKE WON'T EAT!!

This is probably the most common problem with captive snakes. Nearly every time, it is caused by some environmental complaint—usually conditions that are too cold for the snake.

If your snake won't eat, check the temperature in his cage. For most snakes, the daytime temperature should be around 80 degrees, dropping to the mid 70s at night. Make sure your snake has a basking spot of at least 90 degrees.

Also, be sure your snake has a hide box where he can feel safe and secure. Most snakes will not eat if they feel threatened and exposed, and need a dark, confined space where they can curl up and feel protected.

Since most snakes are nocturnal, it may also help to feed your snake at dusk, when it is most active and most likely to be in an eating mood.

One way to tempt a finicky eater is to peel a bit of skin from the nose of its prey, so a little blood or fluid leaks out. The scent of body fluids is a powerful lure for snakes, and may be enough to trigger the feeding response.

Remember that most snakes will refuse food for a period of several weeks before they shed. However, if more than six weeks pass without the snake eating and it has not shed its skin, you should begin to suspect a medical problem, and get the snake to a vet for a checkup.

many people believe, a constricting snake does not crush its prey to death; rather, the snake will tighten its coils every time the prey animal exhales, which squeezes the prey's chest tighter and tighter, until it can no longer inhale and it smothers. Once the prey animal is dead, the snake will use its tongue to examine it until it finds the head, and will then proceed to swallow the prey nose-first.

There are several reasons why it is best for the snake hobbyist to feed pre-killed prey exclusively, but the most important is for the safety of the snake. Mice and other rodents are fast, smart and have lethal teeth. Snakes, on the other hand, are slow, stupid and can only kill by constriction.

If, for whatever reason, the snake decides that it does not want to eat a live food animal, the prey animal is very capable of turning on the snake and killing it. Even if the snake is willing to feed, it will very occasionally make slight mistakes in its attack—it may grab the rodent by the wrong end, or it may miss in its initial strike, and even a slight opening is enough for the mouse to counterattack.

Live mice will fight for their lives when they are seized, and will bite, kick and scratch for as long as they can. Every experienced snake keeper can tell stories of snakes who have been severely bitten and injured by live food animals, and most snake collectors have at least one snake with the scars to prove it.

How to Feed

In most cases, feeding pre-killed food to a snake is a simple matter of dropping a dead mouse or other rodent into the cage and waiting until nature takes its course. If you are using frozen mice, be certain that the mouse is thawed thoroughly all the way through; if the center of the mouse is still frozen when the snake swallows it, it can produce severe intestinal distress that might even kill the snake. One good way to thaw a frozen mouse is to pop it in the microwave for a minute or two on low power (don't tell your housemates you are doing this). Another good method is to place the frozen mouse in a ziplock plastic bag, and then place this in a pan of hot water for about fifteen minutes.

Most snakes will prefer to eat in the dark, just after nightfall, and many snakes will drag their prey into their hide box before swallowing it. Some individuals will prefer to let their prey sit for a few hours before they will eat it. A few snakes may prefer to constrict the dead prey first (apparently to make sure it is dead), but most will simply grab it in their jaws and start swallowing.

Tempting Your Snake

Some snakes, however, may prefer their prey to be moving before they will take it, and this can be accomplished with a pair of long-handled tongs or forceps (never touch a dead mouse with your bare skin when you are feeding a snake; the snake may mistake your hand for a food item and bite you). Using the tongs, hold the mouse by the tail and dangle it gently a few inches from the snake's face.

After a few exploratory tongue flicks, your snake will seize the food and go through the motions of constricting it. If your snake seems reluctant to feed, lightly touching the food item to the snake's nose may be enough to trigger the feeding response.

If your snake repeatedly strikes at the mouse and then quickly withdraws, it means he is not hungry. Try again in a day or so. (Please note that most snakes will stop eating for a period of several weeks before they shed their skin.)

FEEDING DO'S AND DON'TS

Do feed your snake whole mice. They need viscera and stomach contents, too.

Do feed a single species to your snake its entire life.

Do feed pre-killed food, for your convenience and your snake's health.

Do thaw a frozen mouse before feeding.

Do keep a shallow dish of fresh water in the cage at all times.

Don't feed too much or too often: Because of their systems, snakes don't need much food.

Don't handle your snake soon after it's eaten. Give it time to digest its meal in peace.

This snake keeper is tease-feeding a hatchling Snow Corn Snake. First he wiggles the pre-killed prey in his hand, presenting the nose end to the snake. The snake strikes and holds onto the prey. While the snake is swallowing, the handler remains motionless.

Obtaining Food

If you are going to feed live prey animals to your snakes, you have two basic choices for obtaining your food: you can either buy live animals from a pet store, or you can raise your own.

If you absolutely must feed your snakes live food (and remember, my firm advice is that you do *not*), the easiest way is to drive to the pet store and pick up a rat or a rabbit whenever the boa is hungry. (A live rodent will have a higher food value for the snake if you feed it several meals before using it as food.)

Feeding your pet snake pre-killed food exclusively is not only much safer for the snake, but is much easier logistically for the keeper (and is less expensive as well). A number of reptile supply houses sell frozen mice, rabbits and other snake food, in bulk and usually at less than half the price that live prey animals would cost in a pet store. (Several frozen food providers are listed in the Resources section at the end of this book.)

Or, if you have mice in your basement and set out traps for them, consider this a blessing in disguise. When removed from the trap and frozen hard for a few weeks, those household pests can become your snake's next meal.

Besides price, pre-killed frozen snake food has a number of other advantages for the hobbyist. The freezing process will have killed all of the internal and external parasites that may be present in the food animal, thus eliminating the possibility of exposing your snake to mites or worms.

Frozen food can also be easily and conveniently stored until needed. The snake keeper can buy several months' supply of mice at one time, and stack them neatly in the freezer until he or she needs them. (You might want to keep them wrapped in plastic inside a paper bag, though, since your housemates might not like having a number of dead mouse-sicles snuggled up against their Butter Brickle ice cream.)

Also, if a snake is not hungry and refuses to eat a live rodent, the keeper is faced with the task of keeping the food animal somewhere until the snake is ready for it; a frozen and thawed mouse, however, can simply be popped into the refrigerator for a few days until it is needed.

Water

All snakes, even those from the most arid of desert regions, need access to clean drinking water at all times. Snakes drink by submerging their snouts in the water and then using pumping motions in the throat to suck water in before raising the head to swallow.

Because most snakes are active at night, you are unlikely to see your snake actually drinking, but he will be taking a nip now and again whenever he needs it—particularly after he eats.

Incidentally, it is a good idea not to handle a snake that has just eaten or taken a drink, as the pressure of your hands on the snake's stomach may be enough to cause it to vomit.

Because the water dish is also necessary to keep an acceptable humidity level, and because snakes will often want to soak themselves just before a shed, the water pan in a snake's cage should be large enough for the snake to submerge itself completely. Commercially available water dishes, which are molded out of plastic and made to look like natural rocks, are acceptable. In a pinch, however, any large flat dish that cannot be tipped over will do.

Many snakes have an annoying habit of defecating in their water dish. If yours does this, there is not much you can do to break it of the habit; just be sure and replace the water as soon as it is fouled.

chapter 6

Handling
Your
Snake

One of the joys of snake keeping is the opportunity to handle these alert and curious animals, allowing you to admire their unique beauty at close range. All snake keepers must learn how to properly handle snakes, since it will be necessary to do so in order to perform tasks such as cleaning the cage and visiting the vet.

Handling a big boid is a job that should not be attempted alone. A ten-foot python can easily weigh over one-hundred pounds, and if a snake that size decides to rough you up a bit, there is not much you will be able to do to stop him by yourself. Also, if the snake decides to coil you and begin constricting, you will need somebody—very quickly—to help get him off you. The safest way to handle a big boid is for one person to control the head and front end, with another person (or two or three) to support the rest of the body. Needless to say, a big boa or python should be handled as rarely as possible.

Obviously, snakes and infants or toddlers don't mix, and you should keep them separated. Children over five years of age can handle medium-sized snakes if they are taught to do so gently and properly. Children should always be supervised while handling snakes.

If a snake has been handled from the time it's a hatchling, it should be used to it; if not, you'll have to tame it to accept handling, which shouldn't take long if you're slow and steady. (Worm Snake)

Taming Your Snake

If your snake is captive-bred and has been handled properly by the breeder and dealer, it is probably already at least somewhat tamed, and does not view humans as potential threats. Many times, however, commercial breeders and dealers do not have the time to properly handle every snake, and your snake, particularly if it is young, may not yet be accustomed to regular handling. If this is the case, you will have to take on the task of taming the snake yourself.

The only way to accustom a snake to handling is to handle it. If you're not sure how your snake will cooperate, you can be extra careful and wear long sleeves and leather gloves in case it starts to bite. Remember, go slowly, calmly and patiently at all times.

Most often, the toughest part of handling a snake is getting it out of the cage. The cage, and particularly the hide box, is where your snake feels safe and secure, and by reaching into it, you are intruding into his territory and acting in a threatening manner. Naturally, unless he has already learned that humans are not a threat, he will react defensively.

When approaching a snake that has not yet been tamed, you must move calmly and deliberately. Quick motions and sudden grabs are the actions of a predator, and if you approach a snake in that manner, you are very likely to be bitten. Move slowly and allow the snake to see your intentions.

Reach into the tank and gently grasp the snake by the neck, just behind the jaws. This allows you

You should grasp the snake just behind the jaws and support its body while holding it. (Broadbanded Water Snake)

to control the head and prevent the snake from biting. You will be much more successful at this if you approach the snake from as low as possible. Most predators of snakes, such as hawks, attack from above, and the sight of a looming shape coming down at him may be enough to provoke defensive behavior in the snake.

To lift the snake out, gently reach under its body with the other hand. You should not be lifting the snake out by its head, since this can cause it to thrash around and severely injure itself. Snakes have only a single ball-and-socket connection between their skull and their spine, and if you hold a snake by his head with the body unsupported, the slightest jarring motion can pull the spine away from the skull and cause instant death. This is particularly true of the large, heavy bodied boas and

83

pythons, but it can happen with any snake if it thrashes around enough.

When the snake is properly held, the grip on the head should be just tight enough to prevent the snake from turning and biting, while your other hand supports most of the snake's weight.

At this point, the snake may begin writhing vigorously, and may expel the contents of its anal glands. This

is a normal defensive reaction and is to be expected. The important thing to keep in mind is, no matter how messy and unpleasant the snake may become, *do not* put it down yet. If you hurriedly put the snake back into its cage every time it sprays you, it will quickly learn that this trick will get you to leave it alone. Instead, gently restrain the snake's head with one hand while supporting its weight with the other, and allow the snake to wrap its tail around your arm or wrist. After a few minutes, no matter how agitated the snake is, it will tire and calm down. Only when it is lying still is it the time to put it back.

Eventually your snake will feel comfortable enough to wrap itself around you while you're holding it. (Tangerine Honduran Milk Snake)

Regular Contact

If you continue to handle the snake for about fifteen or twenty minutes every day, it will soon learn that you are not a threat, and will lose some of its defensiveness. Within a short time, you will be able to release its head and allow it to go where it wants. Very likely, at first it will want very badly to get to the floor and away from you, and you will need to keep a secure grip on the snake to prevent him from taking off. After some more handling, however, the snake will come to view you as nothing more than a funny-looking tree that moves around an awful lot.

Some snakes may actually seek out human contact and may even seem to "enjoy" being held. While some owners tend to anthropomorphize and attribute human qualities—love, affection, etc.—to the snake, in

reality, besides being solitary animals that do not normally interact socially with other living things, snakes also have rather poorly developed brains, and lack the cerebral hemispheres necessary to produce these emotional states. Thus, snakes are simply not capable of any of the emotions that some owners attribute to them. In most cases, even the snake that "likes to be held" is not really reacting emotionally to the human presence—snakes like to be warm, and a human body is a very warm place indeed to curl up for a while.

Handle your snake daily and it will soon learn people are not a threat.

Let the Snake Be the Guide

Once the snake has become accustomed to being handled, you will do well with him as long as you do not attempt to control the snake's motions. Instead, let him go where he wants to and follow along with your hands to keep supporting him. However, if the snake tries to crawl down your shirt or onto the top of your head (eyeglasses are a favorite perch), gently grasp his neck and maneuver him in another direction. Keep in mind that even tame snakes do not like being touched on the face or head.

While young children are fascinated with snakes and find them irresistible, they should not be allowed to handle small or delicate snakes, as these tend to be too prone to injury to withstand the sometimes rough treatment they get from children. Larger and heavier snakes, however, as long as they have been accustomed to being handled by people, do not mind being handled by small children (always under supervision, of course). My eight-year-old niece enjoys handling my snakes, and the snakes in turn do not mind being picked up, prodded and pulled around by small children, so long as things don't get too rough.

What to Do if You Are Bitten by a Snake

I do not wish to imply in this section that every snake you see will try to bite you. In general, snakes are shy and nonaggressive creatures that tame quickly and easily—you are much more likely to be bitten by a pet hamster than by a pet snake. Nevertheless, like any other animal, snakes will defend themselves if they feel threatened, and it is not impossible that you will be bitten at least once if you keep snakes for any length of time.

Snakes are shy creatures by nature, and aren't prone to biting, though accidents do happen. (Corn Snake)

Generally, as long as the snake is nonvenomous and not very large, you will not need to do anything about the bite. Small snakes such as garters are not strong enough to break the skin, and can do no more damage than a mildly painful pinch.

Larger snakes such as water snakes or bull snakes pack more of a punch, and may be able to break the skin and draw blood. The most unpleasant of all are bites from a big boid, since the sheer force of the bite is painful enough, without the added pleasure of some 200 needle-sharp teeth embedded in your flesh. A solid bite from a big boa or python can cause some nasty lacerations, which may even require stitches to close. Once you are bitten by a large snake, you will not want to ever repeat the experience. Keep in mind, though, that whenever a snake bites you, it is usually your fault—you have either fooled the snake into thinking you are a meal, or you have done something to make the snake feel threatened. (Some snakes are much more easily fooled or threatened than others. That is why, as the alert reader may have noticed, the big boids figure very low in my list of the 10 best species to keep, and very high on my list of the 10 worst.)

Usually, when a snake bites in self-defense, it will immediately release you and recoil for another strike. Sometimes, however, the snake's backward-pointing teeth can become so deeply embedded that the snake cannot easily get them out. If this happens, do *not* try to pull or pry the snake off, or you will definitely lose skin. Instead, you should grasp the snake firmly behind the jaws and push his head *forward*, in the direction of the nose, to disengage the teeth. After this, you

Though your snake may be a gorgeous, tame pet to you, to others it's a dangerous, vicious creature. Take those perceptions seriously before showing off your pet. (Red Amazon Tree Boa)

may have to gently pry the snake's nose to get him to release you. If the snake has mistaken you for food, it may be quite reluctant to let go until it realizes its mistake (I have had water snakes actually try to swallow my finger). If necessary, a quick dunking in some ice cold water will convince the snake to find easier prey.

Once you have the snake off you, wash the wound with some soap and water and then forget about it. Since many snakes, including water snakes and garters, have mild anti-coagulants in their saliva, the wound may bleed freely for several minutes. But unless you have been lacerated by a big boid and need stitches, there is not much to worry about.

chapter 7

Diseases and Problems

In general, snakes are quite hardy animals and, provided they are being kept in proper conditions, they are unlikely ever to present you with urgent medical problems. Captive snakes, however, are subject to a number of ailments, several of which can be life-threatening if not promptly identified and treated.

Taking Your Snake to the Vet

Finding a good veterinarian for your snake may be one of the most difficult tasks you are likely to face. While most vets are heavily trained in small-animal care, only a few have had any training in the unique medical requirements of reptiles and amphibians. As a result, most veterinarians will flatly refuse to examine your snake. Some who will decide to give it a try may have no practical experience whatsoever with reptiles, and very little training beyond a single course or two in herp anatomy and physiology.

How, then, can one find a suitable vet? The first choice is to approach your local herpetological society for help. Not only does your local herp society deal with qualified veterinarians all the time in matters such as adoptions and rescues, but most of the competent reptile vets are likely to be members of the herp society themselves. Another choice, if you have a local wildlife rehabilitation center or zoo nearby, is to ask for their help—they might be able to point you to a good herp vet.

If your snake is maintained under proper conditions, it is unlikely that he will ever need more than an annual checkup from the vet. Problems can arise, however, and the snake hobbyist should be able to recognize the onset of a condition, deal with a minor problem and determine when he needs to get the snake to a vet.

It's important to find a knowledgeable veterinarian for your snake. Your local herp society can help. (This is Dr. Josie Thompson in California.)

Wounds

Wounds are most commonly seen in snakes housed with aggressive cagemates or animals that are being fed live food. Another common cause of wounds is rubbing of the nose against the screen top in an attempt to escape, which may rub the scales raw and lead to infection. Snakes that are improperly housed can also suffer burns, either from inadvertent contact with a basking light, or from a malfunctioning hot rock or sizzle stone.

Smaller wounds and burns can be treated at home by applying an antibiotic ointment such as Neosporin, which is available at any drugstore, to the injury. Snakes have a remarkable natural ability to heal wounds, and, so long as the area is kept clean and is disinfected with antibiotic, it should heal without further attention. If the wound is large or gaping, however, the services of a vet may be needed to stitch it closed.

The best way to prevent burns and wounds is through proper housing. Aggressive snakes that are likely to bite one another should be housed separately. Hot rocks or sizzle stones should not be used, and basking lights must be carefully arranged so that the snake cannot reach them or physically touch them. One of the most common causes of snake wounds is the practice of feeding live prey animals as food.

Make sure your veterinarian checks for signs of mouth rot.

Mouth Rot

Mouth rot, which is known under the technical name of infectious necrotic stomatitis, is a severe condition that is usually the result of an injury to the mouth, teeth or gums. Once the lining of the mouth has been broken by some minor injury, bacteria can invade the wound and multiply, producing a corrosive toxin which eats away the surrounding tissues. This results in a swollen red area inside the mouth, which will continuously slough off dead tissue as well as a cheesy grey pus. The first sign is usually a refusal to eat, and examination of the inside of the mouth will reveal the telltale lesions and encrustation of dead tissue. If untreated, mouth rot will destroy the lining of the mouth and cause death.

You will need a vet to deal with this problem. The vet will swab the infected areas with a disinfectant like hydrogen peroxide, and will also administer vitamin shots and antibiotics to help the snake fight off the infection. The sooner the condition is discovered, the better the chance of complete recovery.

Respiratory Infections

These are probably the most common cause of death among captive snakes. Infected snakes will begin having noticeable difficulty in breathing, and may sneeze or make audible wheezing or bubbling sounds with each breath. Very often, the snake will breathe with its mouth held open. Fluid may leak or bubble from the nose, and the snake may stop eating. If untreated, upper respiratory infections can spread to the lungs, where they will produce pneumonia, which is difficult to treat and will probably be fatal. Upper respiratory infections are highly contagious, and can sweep quickly through an entire reptile collection, infecting nearly every animal.

This problem is the result of a bacterial infection, but it is nearly always brought on by keeping the snake at a temperature that is too low, which leaves the snake's immune system too weak to fight off the invading bacteria. Tropical snakes are vulnerable to respiratory infections if they are chilled for even a short period of time. If it is caught early enough, the infection can usually be cured by improving the snake's conditions and raising the temperature to an acceptably high level (indeed, it may help to keep the temperature a bit higher than normal until the infection clears up). Be sure to quarantine the snake until it is well.

Some snakes will develop respiratory infections if the temperature in their environment drops even a few degrees. (Healthy Eastern Coral Snake)

If the condition doesn't clear up within a week or two, however, or if it is advanced enough that the snake breathes with his mouth open and is refusing to eat, you will need the help of a veterinarian. The vet will prescribe an injectable antibiotic such as tetracycline or baytril, and this will need to be injected every day for a period of several weeks. The vet will show you how to administer the injections, and will supply you with the necessary drugs and syringes. Keep a close eye on the rest of your collection during this time.

Intestinal Infections

The symptoms of an intestinal infection will be obvious and unmistakable. The snake will develop a severe case of diarrhea, and will void watery, slimy feces that will have a powerful odor and may turn a greenish color. If the snake eats at all, it may shortly afterwards vomit up its meal. The culprit is a form of amoeba that attacks the intestinal lining. This is a serious disease and can kill a snake within a very short time. It is also highly contagious and can race rapidly through an entire collection, often with fatal results.

Contributory factors include temperatures that are too low and drinking water that is unsanitary and polluted with feces.

Treatment must begin as early as possible. The vet will begin injections of amoebicides such as Flagyl, and may also administer fluids to fight dehydration.

Another common intestinal problem is the presence of worms or internal parasites. These cannot be detected by an external examination of the snake, but their presence can be indicated if the snake eats normally but never seems to gain weight, or actually becomes thinner. In very heavy infestations, there may be blood present in the feces. If you examine an infected snake's feces, you may be able to see tiny, thread-like worms. Worms are most common in wild-caught snakes.

If you suspect that your snake has worms, your vet will need to see a recent fecal sample. This should be double-bagged in a ziplock baggie—please do *not* freeze the fecal sample before taking it to the vet.

Inclusion Body Disease

This is a very serious (but fortunately somewhat rare) disease, which has only been recently discovered among captive snakes. It is caused by a retrovirus and is invariably fatal (no cure or treatment is known). The disease seems to affect only members of the boid family and, although both boas and pythons are susceptible, boas are more likely than pythons to become "carriers," which harbor the virus but do not show any signs of infection.

Boas and pythons, like this Amethystine Python, are especially susceptible to Inclusion Body Disease.

The disease affects a variety of internal organs, including the kidneys, pancreas and spleen, but the most harm is done to the central nervous system, with serious damage to the brain and spinal cord. Infected snakes therefore show bizarre neurological symptoms such as partial paralysis, inability to turn over, and jerky or uncoordinated motions. Many infected snakes develop an effect known as "star-gazing," in which the muscles of the neck involuntarily contract and pull the head upwards, until it looks as though the snake is looking at the sky. Other symptoms include vomiting and inability to swallow. Infected snakes often cannot shed their skin properly because they cannot control their bodies enough to peel off the old skin. Death comes from paralysis resulting in inability to eat or drink.

Inclusion Body Disease is highly contagious, and appears to be spread through contact with exposed surfaces. The virus may also be spread by snake mites. Infected snakes may not begin to show symptoms until up to six months after exposure.

Since there is no known cure or treatment for Inclusion Body Disease, it is recommended that any infected snakes be removed immediately and humanely euthanized.

Mites and Ticks

Once you've found a veterinarian, make an appointment for a checkup for your snake.

External parasites such as mites and ticks are probably the most commonly encountered health problem among captive snakes. The most obvious signs of infestation are a number of small moving dots on the snake's scales, particularly around the eyes and lips.

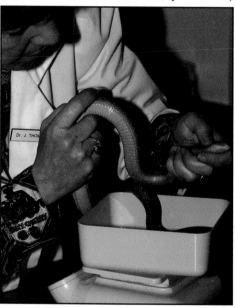

These are snake mites, which are host-specific to snakes—your snake cannot get them from cats or dogs, but only from other snakes or from contact with a surface containing mite eggs. Ticks are a bit larger, and look like small black or brown seeds that are attached between the scales.

Ticks are very common in wild-caught Latin American boids, such as Boa Constrictors and Rainbow Boas. They are also found fairly often in wild-caught Reticulated Pythons. Mites and ticks are both easily transmitted from one cage to another, and may soon spread to infest your entire collection.

Both mites and ticks live by sucking blood from your snake, using their needle-like mouthpieces to pierce the thin skin between the scales. Although this loss of blood will not kill the snake by itself, it does weaken it to the point where it becomes vulnerable to other infections. Ticks and mites themselves can transmit a variety of disease organisms. They should be eliminated as soon as they are detected.

The best way to rid a cage of mites is to use a pest-repellent strip containing the insecticide Vapona. Such strips are readily available at most stores. Place a strip in a cloth bag, remove the water dish from the snake's cage, and place the pest-bag inside for about three days. To kill any newly hatched eggs, this treatment should be repeated a week later.

Ticks are not as vulnerable to the insecticide as are mites, but fortunately there are usually far fewer ticks infesting the snake than mites. The only way to insure removal of ticks is to carefully examine the snake, scale by scale, searching for attached ticks. When one is discovered, it should be dabbed with a drop of alcohol to kill it, and then carefully removed with a pair of tweezers. Great care should be taken to avoid pulling the ticks out too roughly, as this may leave their heads and mouthparts still embedded under the snake's skin, which can lead to an infection.

The best preventative for a mite or tick infestation is carefully to quarantine and examine any new arrivals.

Skin Problems

Most skin problems encountered in snakes will be the result of poor or incomplete shedding.

Before shedding, the snake will usually stop eating and spend most of its time soaking in its water dish. About three weeks later, its skin will get noticeably darker and its eyes will turn a hazy blue as the old outer layer of skin is separated from the inner layer. This blue color will disappear after a few days. About a week after that, the snake will begin to retain fluids in its face, which causes the lips to swell and crack open the old layer of skin. The skin is then pulled off, inside out, in one continuous piece. Snakes will usually shed after having consumed between three and five meals.

Occasionally, snakes have trouble in attaining a complete shed. Boids in particular are prone to peeling their skin off in large flakes instead of one complete piece, which often leaves pieces of old skin still attached. These are excellent breeding places for mites and certain bacteria. They can be removed by spraying the affected areas with a water mister or soaking the snake for several minutes in warm water, and then gently rubbing off the old skin.

This problem usually indicates a humidity level that is too low, and it can be prevented by increasing the moisture content inside the cage. It may also mean that there aren't enough rough areas in the cage for the snake to hook its old skin and peel it off. To prevent this, snake cages should be provided with a pile of rocks and/or some gnarled branches for ease of shedding.

Shed skins should be checked to ensure that the clear eye-cap has been shed properly.

Although incomplete shedding is usually confined to boids, any snake can be affected by another fairly common shedding problem. Snakes lack eyelids, and instead have a clear scale over the eye called the brille or eyecap, which is normally shed along with the rest of the skin during ecdysis. Occasionally, however, the eyecaps become detached from the rest of the skin and are not shed.

Once the eyecap becomes detached in one shed, it tends to continue to remain in place during subsequent sheds. Eventually, these caps build up to the point that the snake can no longer see clearly, which can make it become defensive and irritable. They also serve as breeding grounds for bacteria and ectoparasites. For this reason, it is important to check the discarded skin after every shed to insure that the eyecaps have come off, and are not still attached to the eye.

Water snakes are vulnerable to vitamin B deficiencies when they have a diet consisting solely of fish.

If the eyecap is still attached, it can be removed by soaking the area with a damp cloth for a few minutes, and then carefully lifting it off with a pair of tweezers. If there are several layers of shed built up over the eye, however, a veterinarian should deal with the situation, since improper removal can cause serious and permanent damage to the eyeball.

Captive snakes are also subject to a skin problem that has nothing to do with shedding. This is blister disease, which takes the form of large, fluid-filled blisters underneath the skin, particularly along the belly, which can burst open and become infected. It is most common in garter snakes and water snakes, but is also seen in boids. Usually, blister disease is caused by environmental conditions that are too wet. Treatment consists of placing the snake in drier quarters. If necessary, your veterinarian can provide antiseptics to apply to the blistered areas.

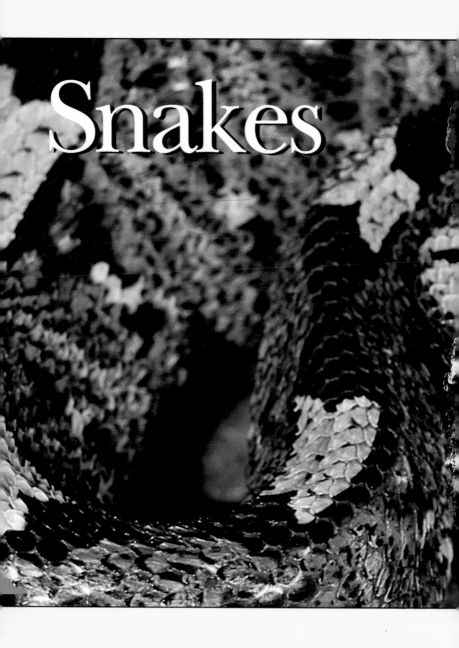

Snakes

part three

in Our

World

chapter 8

Snakes
and the
Law

Until about thirty years ago, there were virtually no laws whatever regulating the capture or sale of wild animals. Individuals or businesses were free, within the limits of the "animal cruelty" laws, to capture whatever species they liked, export or import whatever they wanted, and sell animals to whomever they wished. The unfortunate result was the decimation of many species of wildlife, including reptiles, and the hunting of other species to near-extinction.

In the 1960s and early 1970s, the growing environmental movement made most people aware of the tremendous damage that humans were doing to the ecosystems of our world, and a number of laws were passed to protect threatened or endangered species and to regulate the sale and possession of many types of native wildlife. More recently, as snake keeping has become more and more popular, many local governments have felt a need to pass laws and ordinances regulating the ownership of these animals, in the interests of public safety.

Most of these laws are still in effect, and they may have a direct affect on the amateur snake keeper or hobbyist. Because there are so many differing state and local laws, this book cannot serve as a guide to the legalities of snake keeping. The best it can do is provide a broad overview. It is the responsibility of the individual snake keeper to know and obey all applicable legal restrictions.

This is a Vine Snake from Suriname, which, if it were a CITES species, would be illegal to import or export.

International Laws

Without question, the single most important international agreement affecting snake keepers and hobbyists is the Convention on the International Trade in Endangered Species (CITES), also known as the Washington Treaty, which was signed in 1973 and ratified by the United States in 1975. Over 120 nations have also signed the treaty.

Under CITES, protected animals are divided into two groups. Animals listed under CITES Appendix I are those in immediate danger of extinction. Current

Snakes in
Our World

snakes listed under CITES Appendix I are the Indian Python (*Python molurus molurus*), the Round Island Boa (*Bolyeria multicarinata*), the Round Island Keel-Scaled Boa (*Casarea dussumieri*), the Puerto Rican Boa (*Epicrates inornatus*), the San Francisco Garter Snake (*Thamnopihis sirtalis tetrataenia*), the Central Asian Cobra (*Naja oxiana*), the Latifi's Viper (*Vipera latifii*), the Milos Viper (*Vipera schweizeri*) and the Orsini's Viper (*Vipera ursinii rakosiensi*). It is illegal for anyone except zoos, under special permit, to import or export any of these animals.

THE ENDANGERED SPECIES ACT

The United States passed the Endangered Species Act in 1973. It is a federal law pertaining to the collection and raising of snakes and other reptiles. Its purpose is to conserve ecosystems and species that are endangered or threatened.

Endangered species are those that are in danger of extinction throughout all or a significant portion of their habitat range; threatened species are those that are likely to become endangered within the foreseeable future throughout a significant portion of their range.

Animals listed under CITES Appendix II are not yet in imminent danger of extinction, but are declining rapidly and must be given protection. All of the boids are currently listed under CITES II, including the Burmese Python, the Ball Python, the Boa Constrictor and the Rainbow Boa. It is illegal to import or export any of these species unless they were captured under a special permit, or unless they were bred in captivity.

The primary purpose of the CITES treaty is to prevent the international smuggling of endangered or threatened animals that have been taken from the wild. Wildlife smuggling is a serious problem; according to some Interpol estimates, illegal wildlife trade is a $6-billion-a-year business.

There are several serious flaws in the CITES treaty, however; the most serious is that CITES depends solely on the exporting and importing countries to catch and punish violators. Most imported reptiles come from impoverished Third World nations, which simply do not have the resources to monitor their exports of wildlife. The United States does a fair job of catching violators at this end, but officials here are working with limited resources as well, and the penalties imposed on convicted smugglers are usually little more than a nuisance compared to the enormous profits to be made.

Another problem is that the CITES treaty is binding only if both the exporting nation and the importing nation have signed it. Many Third World nations have not yet signed the treaty. Thus, one easy way around the law is to illegally collect reptiles in one country that has signed the CITES agreement, smuggle them into a neighboring country that has not, and then export them "legally." In the past, this tactic made certain African nations among the largest exporters of Ball pythons—despite the fact that Ball pythons are not indigenous to those nations. To combat this trade, the United States now refuses to allow the import of any CITES-covered species without a permit, whether the nation of origin is a CITES signatory or not.

For all of these reasons, snake hobbyists and collectors should absolutely refuse to buy any imported wild-caught snakes, and should not purchase any snake that was not captive-bred here in the United States.

This woman is holding a tame Everglades Rat Snake, not breaking any of the federal laws against capturing wild endangered or threatened species.

Federal Laws

Endangered Species Act: The most important of the federal laws pertaining to the collection and raising of snakes and other reptiles is the Endangered Species Act, which was passed in 1973, shortly after the CITES treaty was signed. The stated purpose of the Endangered Species Act is "(1) to provide a means whereby the ecosystems upon which endangered species depend may be conserved, [and] (2) to provide a program for the conservation of such endangered and threatened species."

Under the ESA, animals (and plants) that are vulnerable to extinction are listed in two categories. The most vulnerable are listed as "endangered species," which are defined as "any species which is in danger of extinction throughout all or a significant portion of its range." The snakes currently listed as "endangered" are the San Francisco Garter Snake, the Puerto Rican Boa, the Mona Boa, and the Virgin Islands Tree Boa. It is illegal to disturb, collect, possess or sell any of these species.

The corn snake is widely distributed in the southeastern U.S., but isolated in New Jersey, where it is legally protected. (Okeetee Corn Snake)

Organisms that are not yet endangered but which could become so in the near future are classified as "threatened," which defines "any species which is likely to become an endangered species within the foreseeable future throughout all of a significant portion of its range." This category currently includes the Eastern Indigo Snake, the Concho Water Snake and the Atlantic Salt Marsh Water Snake. Threatened species may be collected, captive bred and sold, but only under stringent permits which specify the legal limits on such collection. Anyone in possession of a threatened species should be able to show that the animal was obtained legally.

The only circumstances under which the Endangered Species Act are likely to apply to most snake collectors is if they capture their own snakes in the wild, or if they purchase a snake that is listed as "threatened" or "endangered" from a breeder. Most responsible snake keepers will refrain from collecting wild snakes at all, preferring to keep them in the wild where they belong, and instead buy captive-bred snakes. If, however, you do choose to capture a snake from the wild, be absolutely positive that it is not a species that is protected under the Endangered Species Act. If you purchase a species that is listed under the ESA (Eastern Indigo Snakes, for instance, are listed as "threatened," but can be legally captive-bred and sold under license and sometimes appear on dealers' lists), be sure to ask for the appropriate documentation to show that your snake was obtained legally. Any legitimate breeder of endangered or threatened species will do this routinely.

State Laws

State laws affecting reptile keepers fall into two distinct categories: laws that regulate and control the capture and sale of native species, and laws that regulate or limit the types and number of snakes that may be kept within the borders of that state.

For the most part, laws pertaining to the collection of native snakes are enforced by the state game or wildlife commissions. In most instances, the various states follow a classification system similar to that of the Federal Endangered Species Act. Animals that are in imminent danger of extinction within the state are classified as "endangered species," while animals that are severely declining and could shortly be in danger are listed as "threatened species." In most states, the collection, sale or possession of any endangered species is illegal. The collection and sale of any threatened species is illegal without a permit; the possession of any threatened species is illegal unless it was obtained legally.

WHAT IS CITES?

CITES stands for the Convention on the International Trade in Endangered Species. It is an international agreement known also as the Washington Treaty, signed by over 120 nations and ratified by the U.S. in 1975.

CITES protects endangered species, both those in immediate danger of extinction (CITES Appendix I) and those whose numbers are declining (CITES Appendix II). It is illegal for anyone to import or export CITES Appendix I species, except zoos with special permits. It is illegal for anyone to import or export CITES Appendix II species unless they were captured by special permit or were bred in captivity.

Since the species is only considered within the state's borders, it is entirely possible that any particular species can be listed as "endangered" in one state, and only listed as "threatened" or perhaps not even listed at all in another. The corn snake, for instance, is a widely distributed snake common throughout the southeastern United States, but it also has an isolated population in New Jersey, where it is legally protected.

Being a responsible snake owner involves learning the laws of your home state and any state you plan to travel in.

It is up to you to learn the laws of your home state and any state you will be traveling through. Some states, like Hawaii, will confiscate and destroy your snake if they discover it.

There is good reason for such a drastic measure, however. There are no snakes indigenous to Hawaii, which means that none of the state's native bird life has any natural defense against these predators. If a non-native snake were to be introduced and establish a breeding population, it would quickly wipe out most, if not all, of the unique Hawaiian bird life, much of which is already threatened or endangered.

Such an unfortunate scenario has already taken place on Guam, where the Brown Tree Snake, a rather common species from the South Pacific, was accidentally introduced a few years ago. The snake has now spread over the island and has wiped out a number of unique species of birds, and is threatening to wipe out the rest. By outlawing the importation of snakes, Hawaii is hoping to avoid a similar situation.

Besides state game laws, there is another area of state law that can present snake owners with a legal minefield—liability statutes. In nearly every state, snakes will be considered under the same liability laws as dogs, which means that the owner will be legally liable for any and all actions taken by the snake—including liability for any damages.

Consider carefully what this means. If you are walking through the park with your bull snake and a little kid runs up to the snake, startles it and is bitten, *you* may be legally liable for all of the medical costs. You may also be liable for any punitive damages, pain and suffering, emotional distress or whatever else a good lawyer can dream up. Large boids in particular are likely to be treated under the law as "vicious animals," the legal theory being that the owner of such an animal should have foreseen that it was likely to bite or attack someone. This provision not only increases the odds that you will be sued (and perhaps charged with some criminal offense or another), but it virtually guarantees that any boid that bites a person will be confiscated and probably destroyed.

More and more local laws are being passed against the keeping of large snakes, usually as a result of public outcry over an irresponsible owner's actions. (Mangrove Snake)

Furthermore, since "damages" means any harm or injury inflicted by the presence of the snake, you can be held legally liable for damages even if your snake does not actually physically strike at or bite anyone. In a case that quickly became famous among snake keepers, a python owner was sued and found liable for damages because, while he was carrying the snake around in a public place, a person with acute fear of snakes saw it, became extremely distressed and had a heart attack.

Local Ordinances

While federal and state laws deal largely with conservation issues and regulate the collection and sale of snake species, local municipal and county governments tend to be more concerned with public safety issues. A large number of county or municipal governments have local ordinances that may place limits on the type of snakes hobbyists may keep, in the interests of protecting the public.

A large number of local governments will have ordinances banning the possession of venomous species of snakes. Those that do not have such a law usually pass one quickly if anyone makes the news after being bitten by their pet Puff Adder or cobra. In some of these jurisdictions, exceptions may be made if the snake has been surgically devenomed. In others, however, it will make no difference.

An increasing number of local governments are also passing laws forbidding the possession of any snake larger than eight or ten feet in length, or banning all of the various species of boids, regardless of length. As with the case of venomous snakes, these laws are usually made in response to public outcry after some incident involving a large snake.

From the descriptions and warnings given in this chapter, it may seem as though, in addition to finding a

good vet, snake owners should also make sure they
have a good lawyer on retainer at all times. In reality,
legal problems involving snakes are quite rare. As long
as you act sensibly and take ordinary precautions with
your snakes—don't collect snakes from the wild, don't
buy or sell any snakes you know are endangered or
threatened (unless you have certain proof they were
obtained legally), don't take your snakes out in public,
and above all, don't ever do any stupid macho showing
off with your snakes—it is extremely unlikely that you
will ever run into any legal troubles because of them.

chapter 9

Conservation
of
Snakes

In the United States today, over half a dozen snakes are listed by the federal government as "threatened" or "endangered," and several dozen more have become threatened in various states. Worldwide, many snakes, including every single member of the large and varied boid family of snakes, are considered "threatened" or "endangered" in the wild, and are vulnerable to extinction. Unfortunately, and to our everlasting shame, nearly all of these species have become endangered through the actions of humans. These actions range from unintentional but foreseeable damage (such as draining, cutting down and "developing" the habitats upon which snakes depend) to the deliberate and malicious (such as the "rattlesnake roundups," which pointlessly kill over a quarter million western rattlesnakes every year).

For the most part, the major conservation groups have
not demonstrated any particular interest in endangered or threatened reptiles. It is an unfortunate fact
that, for most people, the desirability of saving a threatened species is directly proportional to how cute and
fuzzy that species is. One would think that, to a true
conservationist, preserving life—all life—is what is
important. Instead, too many "conservationists" limit
their concern to those animals that are cute, furry and
have big brown eyes, such as harp seals and pandas.
When it comes to Ridge-Nosed Rattlesnakes or San
Francisco Garter Snakes or Eastern Indigo Snakes,
their concern with "pre-
serving life" seems to
take a sudden plunge.

*Rattlesnakes are
threatened by
pointless
"roundups" that
kill many thou-
sands a year.
(Western
Diamond Back
Rattlesnake)*

Fortunately, there are
people fighting to pre-
serve our snake and rep-
tile biodiversity, along
with the rest of our
endangered ecosystems.
And, since the pet trade
has traditionally been a
primary offender in driv-
ing many species to the brink of extinction, it seems
only fitting that today's responsible pet owners and
snake keepers should have important roles to play in
herp conservation. I would like therefore to close this
book with a description of what you, as a responsible
snake keeper, can do to help to preserve and protect
these animals.

Herpetological Societies

The bulk of all herpetological education and conservation work in the United States is done, either
directly or indirectly, by national, state and local herpetological societies. These are nonprofit bodies,
which are formed by groups of private citizens for the
express purpose of furthering public education about
reptiles and amphibians and promoting the conservation of wild herps. Herpetological societies also act to

promote responsible keeping and captive breeding of snakes and other reptiles and amphibians.

To help them meet these goals, herpetological societies carry out a number of tasks. Many herp societies have annual "field surveys," in which volunteer teams will comb wildlife habitats to take a census of the local reptile and amphibian populations. This practice allows researchers to study population trends of various species, and may provide advance warning if populations of certain species are beginning to drop. It also helps state and federal officials monitor the populations of animals that are listed as threatened or endangered.

Members of herpetological societies take their hobby seriously, and are usually well informed about all aspects of herp care. This is the photographer's herp library.

Most herp societies will also work with national conservation groups such as the Nature Conservancy to raise money for the purchase of reptile and amphibian habitats, to maintain them in a natural state and insure that they will not be destroyed by future development. A few of the larger herp societies may even own and maintain their own reptile reserves. (Special mention should be made here of the Mid Atlantic Reptile Show, held annually in Baltimore, Maryland by Tim and Diane Hoen. All of the proceeds from this show go directly towards purchasing habitat in Costa Rica for snakes and other wildlife, and some 800 acres of rainforest habitat have already been secured.)

Herp society members also monitor local pet shops, insuring that any reptiles and amphibians that are offered for sale are being kept in adequate conditions.

The most visible work of herpetological societies, however, is in the area of public education. Most herp societies sponsor talks and shows for the public, at which reptiles and amphibians are exhibited and people are educated about the vital roles that reptiles play in various ecosystems. Speakers are usually made available for school classrooms, Boy Scout troops and other groups or organizations that are interested in reptile and wildlife conservation. State and local herpetological societies may also provide witnesses and information for lawmakers and legislatures that are considering regulations and laws affecting reptiles and their keepers.

Herpetological societies also work hard to insure that all keeping of reptiles in captivity is done safely, responsibly and not in a way that would endanger any wild populations. Through newsletters, meetings, guest lecturers and other methods, herp societies disseminate a large amount of information and advice concerning the captive care and breeding of a wide variety of snakes and other reptiles and amphibians.

Many local herp societies also work closely with local veterinarians, and run "adoption" services, which can provide good homes to herps that have been abandoned, confiscated or seized by local law enforcement or humane society officials, or simply given up for adoption.

I cannot encourage you strongly enough to join your local herpetological society. Although membership in a herpetological society can cost between $15 and $35 per year, it is an investment that is well worth making for any snake enthusiast or hobbyist. Not only do you gain access to a rich source of experience and advice, but you will be helping to play an important role in maintaining and protecting these fascinating and unique creatures.

PROMOTING SNAKE KEEPING

As a snake owner, you are part of the bigger family of herpetologists—in your community, country and the world. Wow! Herpetologists know only too well how misinformed most people are about snakes and how, as a result, they are a threat to the snake's—and the snake keeper's—existence. Not knowing much about snakes, most folks are afraid of them.

For the health of herpetologists, but most especially of snakes, it's important to become knowledgeable about your hobby and your pets and to share that information with others.

This chapter will tell you about a lot of ways you can get involved in the herpetological community, and share your love of your snake(s). Chapter 10 gives you the names and addresses of some national and local herp societies. Check 'em out!

Snakes in
Our World

Giving Talks and Lectures

If there are no herpetological societies in your area, do not despair. Your area still contains at least one usable resource which can help educate the public about the ecological roles played by reptiles and the importance of protecting them. That resource is you.

Probably the most important factor in protecting and preserving reptiles (particularly snakes) is public education. Perhaps no animal on earth has been maligned for so long (and without any good reason) as the snake. Most people have at best only a vague understanding of these animals, and most of what they do "understand" is negative and usually inaccurate. For most people, the only good snake is a dead one, and the only proper action to take, upon seeing a snake in the wild, is to bash it over the head with the nearest rock and thus rid the world of this "dangerous creature."

Our fear of snakes isn't inborn, it's taught, and the best way to overcome it is to learn more about them. (Garter Snake)

No one is born with a fear of snakes; it is something that must be taught. Without exception, I have found that young children, who have not yet learned that they are supposed to be afraid of snakes, find them to be fascinating and irresistible. Whenever I talk to a group of people about snakes, I always ask those who are afraid of them to raise their hands, and then ask them why. No one has yet given me a good reason. Most can't give me any reason at all, beyond, "I don't know—I just am."

Invariably, after I have shown them several snakes, allowed them to touch the animals and examine them closely, and explained how they live and why they may ultimately die, over half of those who initially identified themselves as being "scared to death" will approach me afterwards and ask to hold one of the snakes.

This sort of public education is probably the most important work that any snake hobbyist can do. If you are comfortable with public speaking, use your skills to talk to as many people as you can. Go to grade school classrooms, Bible school classes, Boy Scout troops and local environmental associations. If you don't know the scientific names of your pets, or if you can't identify all of the snakes that are native to Madagascar, or if you can't tell a quadrate bone from a tibia, that's okay. As long as you have an understanding of what an ecosystem is and how it works, and what roles snakes play in them (and I hope this book has helped you toward that understanding), you know all the stuff that is important. Beyond that, it is merely a matter of exposing people to the animals and allowing them to see for themselves the fluid motion, the unique behavior patterns and the dazzling array of colors that make snakes so fascinating. The animals themselves are their own best advertisement.

Captive breeding, done right, is a solid contribution on the part of snake keepers to preserving certain species. (Hatching Jungle Carpet Pythons)

Captive Breeding

One of the most concrete contributions that snake keepers can make to reptile conservation is a vigorous and steady program of captive breeding.

There are two different but important possible goals for a captive breeding program. The first is captive breeding of endangered and threatened reptiles for the ultimate purpose of reintroducing them into the wild. This same type of program is the one that has rescued such seriously endangered animals as the Arabian Oryx, the Przewalski's Horse and the Whooping Crane from almost certain oblivion. (The major difficulty faced by such programs, of course, is the continuing destruction of habitats, which too often means that there is no longer any "wild" left for the animals to be released into.)

This sort of desperate program is, however, not yet necessary for most snakes. With the possible exception of the San Francisco Garter Snake, most snake populations (in the United States, at least) are not yet so severely depleted that they must be augmented with captive-bred individuals, and no state has a current captive release program for any American snake. (In fact, many states specifically forbid release of captive-bred animals, to minimize the introduction of non-native diseases or parasites.)

Though Burmese Pythons are widely available in the pet trade, they are not suitable for beginning hobbyists, since they grow to be over 20 feet long and live 25 years.

The second goal of captive breeding, however, is very much within the scope of the amateur breeder and local herpetological societies. One of the chief threats facing many wild populations of snakes, both within the United States and abroad, is overcollection for the pet trade. Several million live reptiles are imported into the United States each year, nearly all of them wild-caught, and most of them are sold as pets. Few wild populations can withstand that sort of drain for very long.

One partial solution to this problem is to encourage captive breeding of these species, so they can be made available to hobbyists and collectors without the necessity of taking any more animals from the wild. For this reason, responsible captive breeding of many species is to be actively encouraged and supported.

Having said that, however, there are two species of which, at least in my opinion, further captive breeding should be *discouraged.* These are the Burmese Python and the Boa Constrictor. There are two reasons why I believe that the current levels of breeding in these species should not be expanded. The first is simply that there are already more than adequate numbers of these species available, and any further breeding is merely diverting the resources of new breeders away from other species that are not as commonly available and which need to be captive-bred, such as the Green Tree Python or the Rainbow Boa or the Eastern Indigo Snake.

Second, and perhaps more controversially, I would argue that the price on these species has already fallen so low as a result of ready availability due to captive breeding, that they are often purchased as "impulse buys" by people who are unprepared to meet their needs, and who in effect sentence these animals to a long slow death.

Burmese Pythons, in particular, are one of the most widely available animals in the pet trade, yet they are not suitable species for beginning hobbyists. A well cared-for Burmese will live over twenty-five years and reach a length over twenty feet. Yet, despite the fact that thousands of juvenile Burms are sold in the pet trade every year, very few of us know of anyone who has a healthy and happy adult. Nearly all of the juveniles sold as pets die within a short time from improper care. Increased breeding of these animals will only serve to lower the price even more, increasing an already excessive supply and leading to more senseless and preventable deaths.

A captive-bred Woma.

There are, however, several species of snakes that present a serious need for effective captive breeding. The rare Woma, for instance, a member of the boid family, is a strikingly beautiful species that is highly prized by serious collectors. Prices for a breeding pair of Woma can run as high as $10,000. At that price, there will be any number of unscrupulous dealers and importers who will capture these animals illegally and smuggle them here for sale to private collectors. Meanwhile, the number of people in the United States who are actively breeding Womas can be counted on the fingers of one hand.

So long as Womas are not being captive-bred, the demand for them will be met by illegally taking these rare animals out of the wild. If a program of captive breeding were emphasized, however, and more of these captive-bred specimens were to become available, the need for taking any of these animals from the wild would be greatly reduced, and the price would fall to levels at which it would no longer be so profitable to take them illegally. The same could be said of other rare snakes such as Green Tree Pythons, Emerald Tree Boas, Indigo Snakes and Rainbow Boas.

For these and many other species, captive breeding is an urgent priority if they are to be protected in the

Milk snakes are good snakes with which to begin a captive-breeding program.

wild. Of course, many of the most endangered species are difficult to breed. This usually means, however, that we simply do not yet know enough about their biology and habits to duplicate them in captivity. It therefore becomes a priority for serious hobbyists to identify the conditions under which these snakes can be kept and bred. Such knowledge will be vital to protecting and maintaining these species—and serious amateurs are fully capable of discovering and providing such knowledge.

For that reason, I strongly encourage every snake keeper and hobbyist who has been inspired by this book to gain a level of experience and confidence that will allow him or her to undertake captive-breeding research. Start with those species that breed fairly easily but are not commonly bred—milk snakes and pine snakes would be good choices. From there, go on to the more difficult and rare species. For many species, the ability to be bred in captivity may be all that stands between them and extinction.

chapter 10

Resources

Further Reading

Behler, John, and F. Wayne King. *The Audubon Society Field Guide to North American Reptiles and Amphibians.* New York: Alfred A. Knopf, 1979.

Carr, Archie. *The Reptiles, Life Nature Library.* New York: Time, Inc., 1963.

Conant, Roger. *A Field Guide to Reptiles and Amphibians of Eastern and Central North America.* Boston: Houghton Mifflin, 1975.

Kauffield, Charles. *Snakes: The Keeper and the Kept.* New York: Doubleday and Co., 1969; Malabar Fla.: Kreiger Publishing Co., 1995.

Mattison, Chris. *The Care of Reptiles and Amphibians in Captivity.* London: Blandford, 1992.

———. *The Encyclopedia of Snakes.* New York: Facts on File, Inc., 1995.

———. *Keeping and Breeding Snakes.* London: Blandford, 1988.

Parker, H. W. *Snakes: A Natural History.* Ithaca, N.Y.: Cornell University Press, 1977.

Riches, R. J. *Breeding Snakes in Captivity.* Miami, Fla.: Palmetto Publishing Co., 1976.

Rosenfeld, Arthur. *Exotic Pets.* New York: Simon and Schuster, Inc., 1987.

Stebbins, R. C. *A Field Guide to Western Reptiles and Amphibians.* Boston: Houghton Miflin Co., 1966.

Vogel, Zdenek. *Reptiles and Amphibians: Their Care and Behavior.* London: Studio Vista, 1964.

Magazines

Amateur Herpetoculturalist
Wahsatch Alliance of Herpetoculturalists
c/o TAH
P.O. Box 1907
Casper, WY 82602

Captive Breeding
P.O. Box 87100
Canton, MI 48187

Reptile and Amphibian Magazine
RD #3 Box 3709-A
Pottsville, PA 17901

Reptiles
Subscription Dept.
P.O. Box 6040
Mission Viejo, CA 92690

Breeders and Snake Dealers

Desert Serpents Reptiles
John Varney
P.O. Box 17154
Fountain Hills, AZ 85269-7154

Glades Herp
P.O. Box 50911
Fort Meyers, FL 33905

Harford Reptile Breeding Center
Al Zulich
P.O. Box 914
Bel Air, MD 21014-0914

International Reptile Supply
6681 62nd Ave N
Pinellas Park, FL 34665

SerpenCo
Rich Zuchowski
P.O. Box 7547
Tallahassee, FL 32314

Special Care Pet Center
5 West Prospect Ave.
Pittsburgh, PA 15205

VJ's Exotic Reptiles
10 Avenue O (on W. 11th St.)
Brooklyn, NY 11204

Frozen Snake Food

Gourmet Rodent
6115 SW 137th Ave.
Archer, FL 32618

Lam Distributing Company
P.O. Box 407
Rusk, TX 75785

Mouse Trap
P.O. Box 253
Colton, OR 97017

Southwest Rodents
Dave Parizek
13911 S. Old Sonoita Hwy.
Vail, AZ 85641

Special Care Pet Center
5 West Prospect Ave.
Pittsburgh, PA 15205

Suwannee Mouse Farm
P.O. Box 14
Suwannee, FL 32692

National Herpetological Societies and Associations

American Federation of Herpetoculturalists
P.O. Box 300067
Escondido, CA 92030-0067
(Publisher of *The Vivarium.*)

American Society of Icthyologists and Herpetologists
Business Office
P.O. Box 1897
Lawrence, KS 66044-8897
(Publishes the quarterly journal, *Copeia.*)

National Herpetological Alliance
P.O. Box 5143
Chicago, IL 60680-5143

Society for the Study of Reptiles and Amphibians
Karen Toepfer
P.O. Box 626
Hays, KS 67601-0626

Local Herpetological Societies

(This listing is far from complete. If you contact the societies listed below, they may be able to point you to a herp society that is closer to you.)

Fairbanks Herpetocultural Society
Taryn Merdes
P.O. Box 71309
Fairbanks, AK 99707

Arizona Herpetological Association
P.O. Box 39127
Phoenix, AZ 85069-9127

Arkansas Herpetological Association
Glyn Turnipseed
418 N. Fairbanks
Russelville, AR 72801

Northern California Herpetological Society
P.O. Box 1363
Davis, CA 95616-1363

Southern California Herpetology Association
P.O. Box 2932
Sante Fe Springs, CA 90607

Colorado Herpetological Society
P.O. Box 15381
Denver, CO 80215

Southern New England Herpetological Association
470 Durham Rd.
Madison, CT 06443-2060

Delaware Herpetological Society
Ashland Nature Center
Brackenville and Barley Mill Rd.
Hockessin, DE 19707

Central Florida Herpetological Society
P.O. Box 3277
Winter Haven, FL 33881

West Florida Herpetological Society
3055 Panama Rd.
Pensacola, FL 32526

Georgia Herpetological Society
Department of Herpetology, Atlanta Zoo
800 Cherokee Ave. SE
Atlanta, GA 30315

Idaho Herpetological Society
P.O. Box 6329
Boise, ID 83707

Central Illinois Herpetological Society
1125 W Lake Ave.
Peoria, IL 61614

Hoosier Herpetological Society
P.O. Box 40544
Indianapolis, IN 46204

Iowa Herpetological Society
P.O. Box 166
Norwalk, IA 50211

Kansas Herpetological Society
Museum of Natural History, Dyche Hall
University of Kansas
Lawrence, KS 66045

Central Kentucky Herpetological Society
P.O. Box 12227
Lexington, KY 40581-2227

Louisiana Herpetological Society
Museum of Natural History
Foster Hall, LSU
Baton Rouge, LA 70803

Maryland Herpetological Society
Natural History Society
2643 N Charles St.
Baltimore, MD 21218

New England Herpetological Society
P.O. Box 1082
Boston, MA 02103

Michigan Society of Herpetologists
321 W. Oakland
Lansing, MI 48906

Minnesota Herpetological Society
Bell Museum of Natural History
10 Church St SE
Minneapolis, MN 55455-0104

Southern Mississippi Herpetological Society
P.O. Box 1685
Ocean Springs, MS 39564

St. Louis Herpetological Society
Harry Steinmann
P.O. Box 220153
Kirkwood, MO 63122

Northern Nevada Herpetological Society
Don Bloomer
P.O. Box 21282
Reno, NV 89502-1282

Association for the Conservation of Turtles
and Tortoises
RD 4, Box 368
Sussex, NJ 07461

New Mexico Herpetological Society
University of New Mexico
Department of Biology
Albuquerque, NM 87131

New York Herpetological Society
P.O. Box 1245
Grand Central Station
New York, NY 10163-1245

North Carolina Herpetological Society
State Museum
P.O. Box 29555
Raleigh, NC 27626

Central Ohio Herpetological Society
217 E. New England Ave.
Worthington, OH 43085

Northern Ohio Association of Herpetologists
Department of Biology
Case Western Reserve University
Cleveland, OH 44106

Oklahoma Herpetological Society
Tulsa Chapter
5701 E. 36th St. N
Tulsa, OK 74115

Oklahoma Herpetological Society
Oklahoma City Chapter
Oklahoma Zoo
2101 NE 50th
Oklahoma City, OK 73111

Oregon Herpetological Society
WISTEC
P.O. Box 1518
Eugene, OR 97440

Snakes in
Our World

Lehigh Valley Herpetological Society
Rich Rosevear
P.O. Box 9171
Allentown, PA 18105-9171

Philadelphia Herpetological Society
Mark Miller
P.O. Box 52261
Philadelphia, PA 19115

Pittsburgh Herpetological Society
Pittsburgh Zoo
1 Hill Rd.
Pittsburgh, PA 15206

Rhode Island Herpetological Association
30 Metropolitan Rd.
Providence, RI 02909

South Carolina Herpetological Society
James L. Knight
P.O. Box 100107
Columbia, SC 29230

Texas Herpetological Society
Hutchinson Hall of Science
31st at Canton
Lubbock, TX 79410

Utah Herpetological Society
Hogle Zoo
P.O. Box 8475
Salt Lake City, UT 84108

Washington Herpetological Society
12420 Rock Ridge Rd.
Herndon, VA 22070

Pacific Northwest Herpetological Society
P.O. Box 70231
Bellevue, WA 98008

Wisconsin Herpetological Society
P.O. Box 366
Germantown, WI 53022